This edition is a comprehensive selection from the whole of *The Federalist,* giving full scope to the authors' political ideas and their meaning for American democracy today. Based on an authoritative text of the original, each selection included is complete and unabridged.

Andrew Hacker is a graduate of Amherst College, Oxford University, and Princeton University, where he received his PhD in 1955. He is currently Professor of Government at Cornell University. He has written several important books and numerous articles on politics and political science.

☆☆☆☆☆☆☆☆☆☆☆☆☆☆☆☆☆☆☆☆☆☆☆☆☆☆☆☆

THE
Federalist
Papers

☆☆☆☆☆☆☆☆☆☆☆☆☆☆☆☆☆☆☆☆☆☆☆☆☆☆☆☆

Selected and with an
Introduction by Andrew Hacker

☆☆☆☆☆☆☆☆☆☆☆☆☆☆☆☆☆☆☆☆☆☆☆☆☆☆☆☆

WASHINGTON SQUARE PRESS
POCKET BOOKS • NEW YORK

THE FEDERALIST PAPERS

The Federalist was first published in serial form, 1787-88, by J. and A. M'lean, New York.

WASHINGTON SQUARE PRESS edition published March, 1964
8th printing.....................February, 1977

Published by
POCKET BOOKS, a division of Simon & Schuster, Inc.,
A GULF+WESTERN COMPANY
630 Fifth Avenue, New York, N.Y. 10020.

WASHINGTON SQUARE PRESS editions are distributed in the U.S. by Simon & Schuster, Inc., 630 Fifth Avenue, New York, N.Y. 10020, and in Canada by Simon & Schuster of Canada, Ltd., Markham, Ontario, Canada.

Table of Contents

Introduction

When the Constitutional Convention adjourned at the end of the summer of 1787, the delegates returned to their own states realizing that their job was only partly completed. The second step was to embark upon a series of grassroots campaigns that would secure ratification of the document over which they had labored in Philadelphia.

THE FEDERALIST and Its Audience. Most memorable of these campaigners were Alexander Hamilton, James Madison and John Jay. Returning to New York, territory not entirely hospitable to the proposed Constitution, they decided that the newspapers were the best means of bringing their case to the largest number of people. In the fall of 1787, therefore, there began to appear in the *New York Packet* and other papers a series of articles signed by an anonymous "Publius." Continuing through the summer of 1788, the series ran into 85 installments and attempted to describe, explain and justify every article, section and clause of the Constitution. Hamilton and Madison wrote most of the articles, with Jay contributing only five and these dealing mainly with foreign affairs.

If one opens at random to any one of the *Federalist* papers and simply reads the first paragraph that strikes the eye, it is difficult to believe that these words were originally penned for a general readership. Not only is the style elegant in tone, but the level of discourse is pitched at a surprisingly high level. The articles, it will be recalled, were aimed at the average voter— the kind of citizen who today might scan a newspaper over his breakfast table or while commuting to work. Certainly there was far less formal education at that time than there is now. Yet the *Federalist* authors felt free to discuss complex philosophical and sociological questions, to quote serious writers such as Hume and Montesquieu, and to refer to the political experience of Ancient Rome and the Venetian Republic. Hamilton, Madison and Jay talked up to their readers rather than down to them, and if their arguments were intended as propaganda for the Constitution, they avoided emotion-laden symbols, deciding that if ratification was to be secured it should be on the basis of a reasoned case.

It is worth taking a moment to speculate on what has happened in the past 175 years. Literacy and schooling now embrace a greater portion of the population than in 1788, yet the level of political rhetoric is clearly lower than it was at the birth of the Republic. If a new Constitution were to be prepared today, the *Federalist* articles used to gain support for it would probably contain Madison Avenue slogans printed on slick paper with a garland of glossy photographs. The modern public, it would be assumed, is too busy to be bothered with detailed analysis. At best it would be willing to watch a debate on television, so long as the format was suitably entertaining, enlivened perhaps by ready-made questions coming from a panel of newspapermen. The political public quite clearly is not what it once was, and the change has not been for the better. The authors of the *Federalist*, however, would not have been surprised by this decline in popular sophistication, for they had a good grasp of the limitations of human nature.

THE FEDERALIST on Human Nature. The framers of the Constitution had not spent the summer of 1787 on a scholastic exercise. On the contrary, the document they drafted was a practical outline for a government that would have to solve real problems and deal with real people. "If men were angels, no government would be necessary," Madison wrote in No. 51. But both he and Hamilton knew full well that men were far from angelic. Individuals might be generous and kind in their private affairs, but when they entered the political arena a less praiseworthy side of their nature rose to the surface. A person could be quite reasonable when isolated from others— as, for example, when reading one of the *Federalist* papers— but as soon as he was thrown into a group situation he might exhibit irrational attitudes that were previously suppressed. These tendencies, moreover, can be possessed by those on both sides of an issue. "Ambition, avarice, personal animosity, party opposition, and many other motives not more laudable than these," Hamilton wrote in No. 1, "are apt to operate as well upon those who support as those who oppose the right side of a question."

Ambition, avarice and animosity might not have been a complete description of human nature, but it was a safe one. Man, or at least political man, is a creature possessing interests to which he has both a material and an emotional attachment. These interests and the attitudes they engender cannot be abolished by exhortation or education. The *Federalist* authors therefore proceeded on the wise assumption that government must not simply contain the vagaries of self-interest, but should harness them in its attempt to secure the general welfare.

THE FEDERALIST on National Power. The Philadelphia Convention had come together because of growing sentiment that thirteen separate states, loosely joined by the Articles of Confederation, could not muster the resources required to deal with what were clearly national problems. Indeed, many Americans were beginning to think and feel that the United States was (not "were") a single nation and ought properly to have a government uniting the states and their inhabitants. Hamilton was particularly nationalistic, not least because he saw the disunited states as prey to foreign aggression. "Under a vigorous national government," he wrote in No. 11, "the natural strength and resources of the country, directed to a common interest, would baffle all the combinations of European jealousy to restrain our growth." With British power to the North, France in the West, and Spain on the South, it was plain that the young nation saw itself as encircled and ill-prepared to ward off attacks.

This was only one of Hamilton's concerns. Shays' Rebellion in Massachusetts had shown that law and order could not necessarily be safeguarded by the individual states. "A firm union will be of the utmost moment to the peace and liberty of the states as a barrier against domestic faction and insurrection," he wrote in No. 9. This fear of popular uprisings was conservative in emphasis, seeing overzealous public participation as a threat to political stability. Hamilton was quite ready to marshal national power against those who would defy national law. Later on, as Secretary of the Treasury, he used this power to quash the Whisky Rebellion, for he knew that the new nation had to have a firm legal basis if it were to prosper in other areas.

Foremost among these was to be a national, and eventually an industrial, economy. In No. 11 he saw the government as encouraging "an active commerce, an extensive navigation, and a flourishing marine" as a means of underwriting economic growth and laying the foundation for domestic and foreign investment. Indeed, national power, law and order were, in Hamilton's eyes, prerequisites for unleashing the great economic and technological potentialities of the new country. The freedoms he wanted the government to safeguard were those of the entrepreneur to invest in a sympathetic environment, of the businessman to enter into contracts knowing they would be honored, and of the property-owner to feel that his holdings will remain secure. Only if those rights were established would a strong industrialized continent emerge from what was then an agricultural seaboard.

THE FEDERALIST on Democracy. Both Hamilton and Madison, the latter to a lesser degree, were distrustful of democracy. While assuming no small amount of intelligence and sophistication on the part of those who read their articles, they were nevertheless anxious over what might occur if the public were permitted too much power. Neither of the *Federalist* authors was a proponent of popular self-government. They saw America as a republic, not a democracy, with government in the hands of men removed from the general citizenry. This arrangement, Madison wrote in No. 10, would "refine and enlarge the public views by passing them through the medium of a chosen body of citizens, whose wisdom may best discern the true interest of their country and whose patriotism and love of justice will be least likely to sacrifice it to temporary or partial considerations." Such a view was of course consonant with the earlier reflections on the frailties of human nature. Yet there was now added the qualification, a not unimportant one, that there are in society a few individuals less apt than their fellow citizens to be captive to the emotions and interests that can jeopardize the common good.

But would the average American be sufficiently deferential to permit himself to be governed by his betters? Voters are often not a little arrogant, calling for policies that strike them as appealing or for candidates who reflect their prejudices. Yet the republican form must be based on at least some modicum of deference, and Hamilton could only suggest that ordinary citizens are not unaware of their limitations. In No. 35 he wrote: "They are sensible that their habits in life have not been such as to give them those acquired endowments, without which in a deliberative assembly the greatest natural abilities are for the most part useless." Was this a safe expectation upon which to operate? The answer lay partly on whether those holding office would gain the consent of the public by enacting policies accommodating the needs and sentiments of the average man. Wisdom and education would have to be combined with a sensitivity for the basic hopes and fears that stir the popular mind.

THE FEDERALIST on Limited Government. One of the fears prevailing in 1788 was the anxiety lest the new national government, with its accretion of authority under the Constitution, submerge the states. Not only had the thirteen states been independent entities since 1776, but most of them had colonial histories going back for over a century. Loyalties to the states were strongly held, and state governments had developed powers and identities of their own. The *Federalist* papers, therefore, sought to demonstrate on the one hand that the over-all political system would be one under which state and national institutions would divide authority; and on the other that even the scope of the national government would be limited because of the self-restraining manner in which its agencies were arranged. The former safeguard has come to be called "federalism," and the latter the "separation of powers."

Again and again Madison pointed out—for this part of the case fell to him more than to Hamilton—that the powers of the federal government were carefully enumerated in the new Constitution. In fact one of the virtues of such a document was that it gave an explicit rendering of where various political functions were to be performed. An examination of this allocation between state and national jurisdictions, Madison concluded in No. 45, demonstrated that those wedded to the doctrine of States' rights had nothing to fear. "The powers delegated by the proposed Constitution to the federal government are few and defined," he wrote. "Those which are to remain in the state governments are numerous and indefinite." If federalism was a compromise, he implied, the states were the greater beneficiaries.

On top of this the national government would not be a monolithic structure. Not only would the legislative, executive and judicial functions be performed by separate branches, but each would be able to check the excessive or ill-advised actions of the others. Concentrated power had to be avoided if freedom were to be ensured. "No political truth is certainly of greater intrinsic value, or is stamped with the authority of more enlightened patrons of liberty," Madison wrote in No. 47, "than that . . . the accumulation of all powers, legislative, executive, and judiciary, in the same hands . . . may justly be pronounced the very definition of tyranny." Undivided power may lead to tyranny, but the separation of powers can lead to stalemate, inaction and eventual deadlock. Both are undesirable and the constant task of government in a free society is to determine where lies the path between these two extremes.

This problem was contained within the very pages of the *Federalist,* for Hamilton had called for the vigorous use of national power in a wide variety of areas. If the nation was to have an active and coherent policy of encouraging industrial growth, for example, then it could not afford a legislative-executive conflict that would bring the wheels of government to a halt. Yet Madison's emphasis on separated powers and mutual checks and balances might achieve just this effect. It emerges that Hamilton wanted more vigor and power in the national government, especially in the executive branch, than did his co-author. Some attention, then, should be given to the political goals that Madison thought the Republic should pursue.

THE FEDERALIST on Society. If Hamilton tended at times to play the part of the economist, Madison's leaning was in the direction of sociology. He realized that free government must have roots in a society that will allow many forms of human expression. His comments on the sinful character of man made clear his unwillingness to place his trust in altruistic motives or disinterested behavior on the part of individuals. Freedom, then, would have to have a social foundation, and the political process would reflect society even as it sought to direct it.

Madison's conception of American society, moreover, was one where conflict rather than consensus would prevail. The population would be divided into many groups, parties and factions, all struggling to secure benefits they felt to be rightfully theirs. The chief causes of this factionalism, Madison wrote in No. 10, are economic in origin: "The most common and durable source of factions has been the various and unequal distribution of property. Those who hold and those who are without property have ever formed distinct interests in society. Those who are creditors and those who are debtors fall under a like discrimination. A landed interest, a manufacturing interest, a mercantile interest, a moneyed interest, with many lesser interests, grow up of necessity in civilized nations, and divide them into different classes, actuated by different sentiments and views."

From one vantage point Madison was a "premature Marxist," perceiving a class struggle based on different degrees and types of property holdings. From another he was simply describing what we now call "pluralism," a society broken into many groups and interests, all of which pursue their separate goals. Both of these interpretations are valid, but Madison departed from Marx in No. 10, when he declared that government must take a positive role in refereeing and even regulating these warring groups. "The regulation of these various and interfering interests," he said, "forms the principal task of modern legislation." This suggests that the government must have a standpoint of its own—the general welfare—and that it must ensure that special interests are not permitted to aggrandize themselves at the expense of the common good.

THE FEDERALIST on Freedom. Yet factionalism serves a function. If Hamilton and Madison were hostile to democracy it was because they feared that majority rule might turn into majority tyranny. Hamilton's chief prescription was to remove the public as far as possible from the decision-making processes of government. Madison, on the other hand, had a different remedy. It was theoretically true, he granted, that a single-minded majority could use its power to tyrannize individuals or minority groups. But in actual practice the majority need not be single-minded; indeed it may well be that there is no such thing as the "majority" at all.

"Society itself will be broken into so many parts, interests, and classes of citizens," Madison wrote in No. 51, "that the rights of individuals or of the minority, will be in little danger from interested combinations of the majority." The America that Madison saw was, then, actually a composite of many minorities based on various interests and factional groupings. Such majorities as would be formed would be transitory coalitions organized for specific purposes and not likely to persist in the face of new issues. Thus minority rights would be preserved because no minority would be subjected to unrelenting victimization. On the contrary, all minorities would at one time or another be part of a majority coalition. Finally, out of self-interest, all groups would be tolerant when they had the upper hand for they would never know when they would be on the short end of the balloting.

Hence Madison could conclude No. 51 by saying that "a coalition of a majority of the whole society could seldom take place on any other principles than those of justice and the general good." The implication is that political pluralism, like the free market economy, is guided by an Invisible Hand. Self-interested factions will inevitably pursue their special goals and no amount of exhortation will persuade them to work for the general interest. This is the way human nature is constructed, and society is bound to reflect this tendency. However, the interplay of interest groups can temper the excesses of majority rule and in so doing protect minority freedoms. Thus freedom is dependent on a social pluralism and the fragmentation of power among many groups. Indeed, freedom is an unplanned consequence of factionalism and an important reason why the struggle among conflicting interests should be allowed to run its own course.

THE FEDERALIST'S Two Authors. Is the *Federalist* a "split personality," as at least one commentator has suggested? It is certainly true that Hamilton and Madison differed in direction and emphasis on a number of vital issues. Both were republicans rather than democrats, and both took a rather pessimistic view of human nature. But after that they were often at odds with each other. Hamilton, for example, hoped to see an active and powerful national government with a purposeful executive. This power and activity, he felt, should be directed at establishing national prestige in foreign relations, achieving order on the domestic scene and encouraging the growth of an industrial economy. If he talked about freedom, which for the most part he did not, he meant the freedom of the businessman to embark on new and productive ventures. Madison, in contrast, was not as happy about concentrated national power and he wished to see the functions and identities of the states preserved. While at times he felt the government should have coherent policies of its own, at others he saw it as a neutral referee standing among competing groups. Freedom to his mind was the freedom of expression—the rights of speech, press, association, worship—and ought to be guaranteed to all citizens regardless of their economic standing. While he felt that property rights were important he cherished other freedoms as well.

The interesting "split personality," therefore, was not Publius but rather James Madison himself. Alexander Hamilton had made up his mind about what goals the new Republic should pursue and what were the best means of obtaining them. He was on the right side, at least in the sense that our subsequent history has vindicated his vision. Yet the ambiguities of Madison's position have a charm of their own. For in being caught between States' rights and national power, between active and passive government, between property ownership and freedoms of expression, between republican principles and democratic sentiments, he reflected the debates and dialogues most Americans have with themselves. Few of us are so tough-minded as to be unreserved Hamiltonians, even if we grant that such sureness of purpose is necessary for national growth and survival. The Madisonian position, in asking for the best of both worlds, expresses the enduring dilemmas of American political life.

ANDREW HACKER
Ithaca, New York
March, 1963

A SELECTED BIBLIOGRAPHY

This Washington Square Press edition of *The Federalist* is a reprinting of selected papers from John C. Hamilton's edition (Philadelphia: J. B. Lippincott, 1865). Readers who wish to refer to a complete recent edition of *The Federalist* may consult Benjamin F. Wright's edition (Cambridge, Massachusetts: The Belknap Press of Harvard University Press, 1961).

Irving Brant. *James Madison: Father of the Constitution.* Indianapolis: The Bobbs-Merrill Company, 1950.

Gottfried Dietze. *The Federalist: A Classic on Federalism and Free Government.* Baltimore: The Johns Hopkins Press, 1960.

Max Farrand. *The Framing of the Constitution.* New Haven: Yale University Press, 1913.

Louis M. Hacker. *Alexander Hamilton in the American Tradition.* New York: McGraw-Hill Book Company, 1957.

Carl Van Doren. *The Great Rehearsal.* New York: The Viking Press, 1948.

The Federalist Papers

————— *Number 1* —————

Alexander Hamilton

Introduction: The Defects of the Articles of Confederation and the Need for a New Constitution.

After full experience of the insufficiency of the existing Federal Government, you are invited to deliberate upon a new Constitution for the United States of America.

The subject speaks its own importance; comprehending in its consequences, nothing less than the existence of the UNION—the safety and welfare of the parts of which it is composed—the fate of an empire, in many respects, the most interesting in the world. It has been frequently remarked, that, it seems to have been reserved to the people of this country, to decide by their conduct and example, the important question, whether societies of men are really capable or not, of establishing good government from reflection and choice, or whether they are for ever destined to depend, for their political constitutions, on accident and force. If there be any truth in the remark, the crisis, at which we are arrived, may with propriety be regarded as the period when that decision is to be made; and a wrong election of the part we shall act, may, in this view, deserve to be considered as the general misfortune of mankind.

This idea, by adding the inducements of philanthropy to those of patriotism, will heighten the solicitude, which all considerate and good men must feel for the event. Happy will it be if our choice should be directed by a judicious estimate of our true interests, uninfluenced by considerations foreign to the public good. But this is more ardently to be wished for, than seriously to be expected. The plan offered to our deliberations, affects too many particular interests, in-

1

novates upon too many local institutions, not to involve in its discussion a variety of objects extraneous to its merits; and of views, passions, and prejudices, little favorable to the discovery of truth.

Among the most formidable of the obstacles, which the new constitution will have to encounter, may readily be distinguished the obvious interest of a certain class of men in every state, to resist all changes which may hazard a diminution of the power, emolument, and consequence, of the offices they hold under the state establishments: and the perverted ambition of another class of men, who will either hope to aggrandize themselves by the confusions of their country, or will flatter themselves with fairer prospects of elevation from the subdivision of the empire into several partial confederacies, than from its union under one government.

It is not, however, my design to dwell upon observations of this nature. I am aware that it would be disingenuous to resolve indiscriminately the opposition of any set of men into interested or ambitious views, merely because their situations might subject them to suspicion. Candor will oblige us to admit, that even such men may be actuated by upright intentions; and it cannot be doubted, that much of the opposition which has already shown itself, or that may hereafter make its appearance, will spring from sources, blameless at least, if not respectable—the honest errors of minds led astray by preconceived jealousies and fears. So numerous indeed, and so powerful are the causes, which serve to give a false bias to the judgment, that we, upon many occasions, see wise and good men on the wrong as well as on the right side of questions, of the first magnitude to society. This circumstance, if duly attended to, would always furnish a lesson of moderation to those who are engaged in any controversy, however well persuaded of being in the right. And a further reason for caution, in this respect, might be drawn from the reflection, that we are not always sure that those who advocate the truth are actuated by purer principles than their antagonists. Ambition, avarice, personal animosity, party opposition, and many other motives, not more laudable than these, are apt to operate as well upon those who support, as upon those who oppose, the right side of a question. Were there not even these inducements to moderation, nothing could be more ill-judged than that intolerant spirit, which has, at all times, characterized political parties. For, in politics as in religion, it is equally absurd to aim at making proselytes by fire and sword. Heresies in either can rarely be cured by persecution.

And yet, just as these sentiments must appear to candid men, we have already sufficient indications, that it will happen in this, as in all former cases of great national discussion. A torrent of angry and malignant passions will be let loose. To judge from the conduct of the opposite parties, we shall be led to conclude that they will mutually hope to evince the justness of their opinions, and to increase the number of their converts, by the loudness of their declamations and by the bitterness of their invectives. An enlightened zeal for the energy and efficiency of government, will be stigmatized as the offspring of a temper fond of power, and hostile to the principles of liberty. An overscrupulous jealousy of danger to the rights of the people, which is more commonly the fault of the head than of the heart, will be represented as mere pretense and artifice; the stale bait for popularity at the expense of public good. It will be forgotten, on the one hand, that jealousy is the usual concomitant of violent love, and that the noble enthusiasm of liberty is too apt to be infected with a spirit of narrow and illiberal distrust. On the other hand, it will be equally forgotten, that the vigor of government is essential to the security of liberty; that, in the contemplation of a sound and well informed judgment, their interests can never be separated; and that a dangerous ambition more often lurks behind the specious mask of zeal for the rights of the people, than under the forbidding appearances of zeal for the firmness and efficiency of government. History will teach us, that the former has been found a much more certain road to the introduction of despotism than the latter; and that of those men who have overturned the liberties of republics, the greatest number have begun their career by paying an obsequious court to the people, commencing demagogues and ending tyrants.

In the course of the preceding observations it has been my aim, fellow citizens, to put you upon your guard against all attempts, from whatever quarter, to influence your decision in a matter of the utmost moment to your welfare, by any impressions other than those which may result from the evidence of truth. You will, no doubt, at the same time, have collected from the general scope of them, that they proceed from a source not unfriendly to the new constitution. Yes, my countrymen, I own to you, that, after having given it an attentive consideration, I am clearly of opinion, it is your interest to adopt it. I am convinced that this is the safest course for your liberty, your dignity, and your happiness. I affect not reserves, which I do not feel. I will not amuse you with an appearance of deliberation, when I have decided. I frankly acknowledge to you my convictions, and I will freely lay before you the reasons on which they are founded. The consciousness of good intentions disdains ambiguity. I shall not, however, multiply professions on this head. My motives must remain in the depository of my own breast: my arguments will be open to all, and may be judged of by all. They shall at least be offered in a spirit, which will not disgrace the cause of truth.

I propose, in a series of papers to discuss the following interesting particulars . . . *The utility of the UNION to your political prosperity . . . The insufficiency of the present confederation to preserve that Union . . . The necessity of a government, at least equally energetic with the one proposed, to the attainment of this object . . . The conformity of the proposed constitution to the true principles of republican government . . . Its analogy to your own state constitution . . .* and lastly, *The additional security, which its adoption will afford to the preservation of that species of government, to liberty, and to property.*

In the progress of this discussion, I shall endeavor to give a satisfactory answer to all the objections which shall have made their appearance, that may seem to have any claim to attention.

It may perhaps be thought superfluous to offer arguments to prove the utility of the UNION; a point, no doubt, deeply engraved on the hearts of the great body of the people in every state, and one which, it may be imagined, has no adversaries. But the fact is, that we already hear it whispered in the private circles of those who oppose the new constitution, that the Thirteen States are of too great extent for any general system, and that we must of necessity resort to separate confederacies of distinct portions of the whole. This doctrine will, in all probability, be gradually propagated, till it has votaries enough to countenance its open avowal. For nothing can be more evident, to those who are able to take an enlarged view of the subject, than the alternative of an adoption of the constitution, or a dismemberment of the Union. It may therefore be essential to examine particularly the advantages of that Union, the certain evils, and the probable dangers, to which every state will be exposed from its dissolution. This shall accordingly be done.

PUBLIUS.

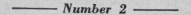

——— *Number 2* ———

John Jay

The Dangers of Foreign Force and Influence Threatening the United States.

When the people of America reflect, that the question now submitted to their determination is one of the most important that has engaged, or can well engage, their attention, the propriety of their taking a very comprehensive, as well as a very serious, view of it, must be evident.

Nothing is more certain than the indispensable necessity of

government; and it is equally undeniable, that whenever and however it is instituted, the people must cede to it some of their natural rights, in order to vest it with requisite powers. It is well worthy of consideration therefore, whether it would conduce more to the interest of the people of America that they should, to all general purposes, be one nation, under one federal government, than that they should divide themselves into separate confederacies, and give to the head of each the same kind of powers which they are advised to place in one national government.

It has until lately been a received and uncontradicted opinion, that the prosperity of the people of America depended on their continuing firmly united; and the wishes, prayers, and efforts, of our best and wisest citizens, have been constantly directed to that object. But politicians now appear, who insist that this opinion is erroneous, and that instead of looking for safety and happiness in union, we ought to seek it in a division of the states into distinct confederacies or sovereignties. However extraordinary this new doctrine may appear, it nevertheless has its advocates; and certain characters who were formerly much opposed to it, are at present of the number. Whatever may be the arguments or inducements, which have wrought this change in the sentiments and declarations of these gentlemen, it certainly would not be wise in the people at large to adopt these new political tenets, without being fully convinced that they are founded in truth and sound policy.

It has often given me pleasure to observe, that independent America was not composed of detached and distant territories, but that one connected, fertile, wide-spreading country, was the portion of our western sons of liberty. Providence has in a particular manner blessed it with a variety of soils and productions, and watered it with innumerable streams, for the delight and accommodation of its inhabitants. A succession of navigable waters forms a kind of chain round its borders, as if to bind it together; while the most noble rivers in the world, running at convenient distances, present them with highways for the easy communication of friendly aids, and the mutual transportation and exchange of their various commodities.

With equal pleasure I have as often taken notice, that Providence has been pleased to give this one connected country to one united people; a people descended from the same ancestors, speaking the same language, professing the same religion, attached to the same principles of government, very similar in their manners and customs, and who, by their joint counsels, arms and efforts, fighting side by side throughout a long and bloody war, have nobly established their general liberty and independence.

This country and this people seem to have been made for each other; and it appears as if it was the design of Providence, that an inheritance so proper and convenient for a band of brethren, united to each other by the strongest ties, should never be split into a number of unsocial, jealous, and alien sovereignties.

Similar sentiments have hitherto prevailed among all orders and denominations of men among us. To all general purposes, we have uniformly been one people. Each individual citizen everywhere enjoying the same national rights, privileges, and protection. As a nation, we have made peace and war: as a nation, we have vanquished our common enemies: as a nation, we have formed alliances and made treaties, and entered into various compacts and conventions with foreign states.

A strong sense of the value and blessings of Union induced the people, at a very early period, to institute a federal government to preserve and perpetuate it. They formed it almost as soon as they had a political existence; nay, at a time, when their habitations were in flames, when many of them were bleeding in the field; and when the progress of hostility and desolation left little room for those calm and mature inquiries and reflections, which must ever precede the formation of a wise and well balanced government for a free people. It is not to be wondered at that a government instituted in times so inauspicious, should on experiment be found greatly deficient, and inadequate to the purpose it was intended to answer.

This intelligent people perceived and regretted these defects. Still continuing no less attached to union, than enamored of liberty, they observed the danger which immediately threat-

ened the former and more remotely the latter; and being persuaded that ample security for both could only be found in a
national government more wisely framed, they, as with one
voice, convened the late Convention at Philadelphia, to take
that important subject under consideration.

This Convention, composed of men who possessed the confidence of the people, and many of whom had become highly
distinguished by their patriotism, virtue, and wisdom, in times
which tried the souls of men, undertook the arduous task. In
the mild season of peace, with minds unoccupied by other
subjects, they passed many months in cool, uninterrupted, and
daily consultations: And finally, without having been awed by
power, or influenced by any passion, except love for their
country, they presented and recommended to the people the
plan produced by their joint and very unanimous counsels.

Admit, for so is the fact, that this plan is only *recommended*,
not imposed, yet, let it be remembered, that it is neither
recommended to *blind* approbation, nor to *blind* reprobation;
but to that sedate and candid consideration, which the magnitude and importance of the subject demand, and which it
certainly ought to receive. But, as has been already remarked,
it is more to be wished than expected that it may be so considered and examined. Experience on a former occasion
teaches us not to be too sanguine in such hopes. It is not yet
forgotten, that well grounded apprehensions of imminent danger induced the people of America to form the memorable
Congress of 1774. That body recommended certain measures
to their constituents, and the event proved their wisdom;
yet it is fresh in our memories how soon the press began to
teem with pamphlets and weekly papers against those very
measures. Not only many of the officers of government who
obeyed the dictates of personal interest, but others from a
mistaken estimate of consequences, from the undue influence
of ancient attachments, or whose ambition aimed at objects
which did not correspond with the public good, were in-
defatigable in their endeavors to persuade the people to reject
the advice of that patriotic Congress. Many indeed were deceived and deluded, but the great majority reasoned and

decided judiciously; and happy they are in reflecting that they did so.

They considered that the Congress was composed of many wise and experienced men. That being convened from different parts of the country, they brought with them and communicated to each other a variety of useful information. That in the course of the time they passed together in inquiring into and discussing the true interests of their country, they must have acquired very accurate knowledge on that head. That they were individually interested in the public liberty and prosperity, and therefore that it was not less their inclination than their duty, to recommend such measures only, as after the most mature deliberation they really thought prudent and advisable.

These and similar considerations then induced the people to rely greatly on the judgment and integrity of the Congress; and they took their advice, notwithstanding the various arts and endeavors used to deter and dissuade them from it. But if the people at large had reason to confide in the men of that Congress, few of whom had then been fully tried or generally known, still greater reason have they now to respect the judgment and advice of the Convention; for it is well known, that some of the most distinguished members of that Congress, who have been since tried and justly approved for patriotism and abilities, and who have grown old in acquiring political information, were also members of this Convention, and carried into it their accumulated knowledge and experience.

It is worthy of remark, that not only the first, but every succeeding Congress, as well as the late Convention, have invariably joined with the people in thinking that the prosperity of America depended on its Union. To preserve and perpetuate it, was the great object of the people in forming that Convention; and it is also the great object of the plan which the Convention has advised them to adopt. With what propriety therefore, or for what good purposes, are attempts at this particular period made, by some men, to depreciate the importance of the Union? or why is it suggested that three or four confederacies would be better than one? I am persuaded in my own mind, that the people have always thought right on this subject, and that their universal and uniform attachment to the cause of the Union rests on great and weighty reasons.

They who promote the idea of substituting a number of distinct confederacies in the room of the plan of the Convention, seem clearly to foresee that the rejection of it would put the continuance of the Union in the utmost jeopardy: that certainly would be the case; and I sincerely wish that it may be as clearly foreseen by every good citizen, that whenever the dissolution of the Union arrives, America will have reason to exclaim in the words of the Poet, "FAREWELL! A LONG FARE-WELL, TO ALL MY GREATNESS!"

PUBLIUS.

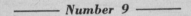

—— *Number 9* ——

Alexander Hamilton

Union as a Safeguard Against Domestic Faction and Insurrection.

A firm Union will be of the utmost moment to the peace and liberty of the states, as a barrier against domestic faction and insurrection.

It is impossible to read the history of the petty republics of Greece and Italy, without feeling sensations of horror and disgust at the distractions with which they were continually agitated, and at the rapid succession of revolutions, by which they were kept perpetually vibrating between the extremes of tyranny and anarchy. If they exhibit occasional calms, these only serve as shortlived contrasts to the furious storms that are to succeed. If now and then intervals of felicity open themselves to view, we behold them with a mixture of regret arising from the reflection, that the pleasing scenes before us are soon to be overwhelmed by the tempestuous waves of sedition and party rage. If momentary rays of glory break forth from the gloom, while they dazzle us with a transient and fleeting brilliancy, they at the same time admonish us to lament, that the vices of government should pervert the direction, and tarnish the luster, of those bright talents and exalted endowments, for which the favored soils that produced them have been so justly celebrated.

From the disorders that disfigure the annals of those republics, the advocates of despotism have drawn arguments, not only against the forms of republican government, but against the very principles of civil liberty. They have decried all free government, as inconsistent with the order of society, and have indulged themselves in malicious exultation over its friends and partisans. Happily for mankind, stupendous fabrics reared on the basis of liberty, which have flourished for ages, have in a few glorious instances refuted their gloomy sophisms. And I trust, America will be the broad and solid foundation of other edifices not less magnificent, which will be equally permanent monuments of their error.

But it is not to be denied, that the portraits they have sketched of republican government, were too just copies of the originals from which they were taken. If it had been found impracticable to have devised models of a more perfect structure, the enlightened friends of liberty would have been obliged to abandon the cause of that species of government as indefensible. The science of politics, however, like most other sciences, has received great improvement. The efficacy of various principles is now well understood, which were either not known at all, or imperfectly known to the ancients. The regular distribution of power into distinct departments; the introduction of legislative balances and checks; the institution of courts composed of judges, holding their offices during good behavior; the representation of the people in the legislature, by deputies of their own election; these are either wholly new discoveries, or have made their principal progress toward perfection in modern times. They are means, and powerful means, by which the excellencies of republican government may be retained, and its imperfections lessened or avoided. To this catalogue of circumstances, that tend to the amelioration of popular systems of civil government, I shall venture, however novel it may appear to some, to add one more, on a principle, which has been made the foundation of an objection to the new constitution; I mean the ENLARGEMENT of the ORBIT within which such systems are to revolve, either in respect to the dimensions of a single state, or to the consolidation of several smaller states into one great confederacy. The latter is that which immediately concerns the object under consideration. It will, however, be of use to examine the principle in its application to a single state, which shall be attended to in another place.

The utility of a confederacy, as well to suppress faction, and to guard the internal tranquillity of states, as to increase their external force and security, is in reality not a new idea. It has been practiced upon in different countries and ages, and has received the sanction of the most approved writers on the subjects of politics. The opponents of the PLAN proposed have with great assiduity cited and circulated the observations of Montesquieu on the necessity of a contracted territory for a republican government. But they seem not to have been apprised of the sentiments of that great man expressed in another part of his work, nor to have adverted to the consequences of the principle to which they subscribe with such ready acquiescence.

When Montesquieu recommends a small extent for republics, the standards he had in view were of dimensions, far short of the limits of almost every one of these states. Neither Virginia, Massachusetts, Pennsylvania, New York, North Carolina, nor Georgia, can by any means be compared with the models from which he reasoned, and to which the terms of his description apply. If we therefore receive his ideas on this point, as the criterion of truth, we shall be driven to the alternative, either of taking refuge at once in the arms of monarchy, or of splitting ourselves into an infinity of little, jealous, clashing, tumultuous commonwealths, the wretched nurseries of unceasing discord, and the miserable objects of universal pity or contempt. Some of the writers, who have come forward on the other side of the question, seem to have been aware of the dilemma; and have even been bold enough to hint at the division of the larger states, as a desirable thing. Such an infatuated policy, such a desperate expedient, might, by the multiplication of petty offices, answer the views of men, who possess not qualifications to extend their influence beyond the narrow circles of personal intrigue; but it could never promote the greatness or happiness of the people of America.

Referring the examination of the principle itself to another place, as has been already mentioned, it will be sufficient to remark here, that in the sense of the author who has been most emphatically quoted upon the occasion, it would only dictate a reduction of the SIZE of the more considerable MEMBERS of the Union; but would not militate against their being all comprehended in one confederate government. And this is the true question, in the discussion of which we are at present interested.

So far are the suggestions of Montesquieu from standing in opposition to a general union of the states, that he explicitly treats of a CONFEDERATE REPUBLIC as the expedient for extending the sphere of popular government, and reconciling the advantages of monarchy with those of republicanism.

"It is very probable," says he, "that mankind would have been obliged, at length, to live constantly under the government of a SINGLE PERSON, had they not contrived a kind of constitution, that has all the internal advantages of a republican, together with the external force of a monarchical government. I mean a CONFEDERATE REPUBLIC.

"This form of government is a convention, by which several smaller *states* agree to become members of a larger *one*, which they intend to form. It is a kind of assemblage of societies, that constitute a new one, capable of increasing by means of new associations, till they arrive to such a degree of power as to be able to provide for the security of the united body.

"A republic of this kind, able to withstand an external force, may support itself without any internal corruption. The form of this society prevents all manner of inconveniences.

"If a single member should attempt to usurp the supreme authority, he could not be supposed to have an equal authority and credit in all the confederate states. Were he to have too great influence over one, this would alarm the rest. Were he to subdue a part, that which would still remain free might oppose him with forces, independent of those which he had usurped, and overpower him before he could be settled in his usurpation.

"Should a popular insurrection happen in one of the confederate states, the others are able to quell it. Should abuses creep into one part, they are reformed by those that remain sound. The state may be destroyed on one side, and not on the other; the confederacy may be dissolved, and the confederates preserve their sovereignty.

"As this government is composed of small republics, it enjoys the internal happiness of each, and with respect to its external situation, it is possessed, by means of the association, of all the advantages of large monarchies."

I have thought it proper to quote at length these interesting passages, because they contain a luminous abridgment of the principal arguments in favor of the Union, and must effectually remove the false impressions, which a misapplication of the other parts of the work was calculated to produce. They have, at the same time, an intimate connection with the more immediate design of this paper; which is to illustrate the tendency of the Union to repress domestic faction and insurrection.

A distinction, more subtle than accurate, has been raised between a *confederacy* and a *consolidation* of the states. The essential characteristic of the first, is said to be the restriction of its authority to the members in their collective capacities, without reaching to the individuals of whom they are composed. It is contended that the national council ought to have no concern with any object of internal administration. An exact equality of suffrage between the members, has also been insisted upon as a leading feature of a confederate government. These positions are, in the main, arbitrary; they are supported neither by principle nor precedent. It has indeed happened, that governments of this kind have generally operated in the manner which the distinction taken notice of supposes to be inherent in their nature; but there have been in most of them extensive exceptions to the practice, which serve to prove, as far as example will go, that there is no absolute rule on the subject. And it will be clearly shown, in the course of this investigation, that, as far as the principle contended for has prevailed, it has been the cause of incurable disorder and imbecility in the government.

The definition of a *confederate republic* seems simply to be, "an assemblage of societies," or an association of two or more states into one state. The extent, modifications, and objects, of the federal authority, are mere matters of discretion. So long as the separate organization of the members be not abolished, so long as it exists by a constitutional necessity for local purposes, though it should be in perfect subordination to the general authority of the Union, it would still be, in fact and in theory, an association of states, or a confederacy. The proposed constitution, so far from implying an abolition of the state governments, makes them constituent parts of the national sovereignty, by allowing them a direct representation in the senate, and leaves in their possession certain exclusive, and very important, portions of the sovereign power. This fully corresponds, in every rational import of the terms, with the idea of a federal government.

In the Lycian confederacy, which consisted of twenty-three CITIES, or republics, the largest were entitled to *three* votes in the COMMON COUNCIL, those of the middle class to *two*, and the smallest to *one*. The COMMON COUNCIL had the appointment of all the judges and magistrates of the respective CITIES. This was certainly the most delicate species of interference in their internal administration; for if there be anything that seems exclusively appropriated to the local jurisdictions, it is the appointment of their own officers. Yet Montesquieu, speaking of this association, says, "Were I to give a model of an excellent confederate republic, it would be that of Lycia." Thus we perceive, that the distinctions insisted upon, were not within the contemplation of this enlightened writer; and we shall be led to conclude, that they are the novel refinements of an erroneous theory.

PUBLIUS.

James Madison

Factions: Their Cause and Control.

Among the numerous advantages promised by a well constructed Union, none deserves to be more accurately developed than its tendency to break and control the violence of faction. The friend of popular governments, never finds himself so much alarmed for their character and fate, as when he contemplates their propensity to this dangerous vice. He will not fail, therefore, to set a due value on any plan which, without violating the principles to which he is attached, provides a proper cure for it. The instability, injustice, and confusion, introduced into the public councils, have, in truth, been the mortal diseases under which popular governments have everywhere perished; as they continue to be the favorite and fruitful topics from which the adversaries to liberty derive their most specious declamations. The valuable improvements made by the American constitutions on the popular models, both ancient and modern, cannot certainly be too much admired; but it would be an unwarrantable partiality, to contend that they have as effectually obviated the danger on this side, as was wished and expected. Complaints are everywhere heard from our most considerate and virtuous citizens, equally the friends of public and private faith, and of public and personal liberty, that our governments are too unstable; that the public good is disregarded in the conflicts of rival parties; and that measures are too often decided, not according to the rules of justice, and the rights of the minor party, but by the superior force of an interested and overbearing majority. However anxiously we may wish that these complaints had no foundation, the evidence of known facts will not permit us to deny that they are in some degree true. It will be found, indeed, on a candid review of our situation, that some of the distresses under which we labor, have been erroneously charged on the operation of our governments; but it will be found, at the same time, that other causes will not alone account for many of our heaviest misfortunes; and, particularly, for that prevailing and increasing distrust of public engagements, and alarm for private rights, which are echoed from one end of the continent to the other. These must be chiefly, if not wholly, effects of the unsteadiness and injustice, with which a factious spirit has tainted our public administrations.

By a faction, I understand a number of citizens, whether amounting to a majority or minority of the whole, who are united and actuated by some common impulse of passion, or of interest, adverse to the rights of other citizens, or to the permanent and aggregate interests of the community.

There are two methods of curing the mischiefs of faction. The one, by removing its causes; the other, by controlling its effects.

There are again two methods of removing the causes of faction. The one, by destroying the liberty which is essential to its existence; the other, by giving to every citizen the same opinions, the same passions, and the same interests.

It could never be more truly said, that of the first remedy, that it was worse than the disease. Liberty is to faction what air is to fire, an aliment, without which it instantly expires. But it would not be a less folly to abolish liberty, which is essential to political life because it nourishes faction, than it would be to wish the annihilation of air, which is essential to animal life, because it imparts to fire its destructive agency.

The second expedient is as impracticable, as the first would be unwise. As long as the reason of man continues fallible, and he is at liberty to exercise it, different opinions will be formed. As long as the connection subsists between his reason and his self-love, his opinions and his passions will have a reciprocal influence on each other; and the former will be objects to which the latter will attach themselves. The diversity in the faculties of men, from which the rights of property originate, is not less an insuperable obstacle to an uniformity of interests. The protection of those faculties is the first object of government. From the protection of different and unequal faculties of acquiring property, the possession of different degrees and kinds of property immediately results; and from the influence of these on the sentiments and views of the respective proprietors, ensues a division of the society into different interests and parties.

The latent causes of faction are thus sown in the nature of man; and we see them everywhere brought into different degrees of activity, according to the different circumstances of civil society. A zeal for different opinions concerning religion, concerning government, and many other points, as well of speculation as of practice; an attachment to different leaders, ambitiously contending for pre-eminence and power; or to persons of other descriptions, whose fortunes have been interesting to the human passions, have, in turn, divided mankind into parties, inflamed them with mutual animosity, and rendered them much more disposed to vex and oppress each other, than to co-operate for their common good. So strong is this propensity of mankind, to fall into mutual animosities, that where no substantial occasion presents itself, the most frivolous and fanciful distinctions have been sufficient to kindle their unfriendly passions, and excite their most violent conflicts. But the most common and durable source of factions has been the various and unequal distribution of property. Those who hold, and those who are without property, have ever formed distinct interests in society. Those who are creditors, and those who are debtors, fall under a like discrimination. A landed interest, a manufacturing interest, a mercantile interest, a moneyed interest, with many lesser interests, grow up of necessity in civilized nations, and divide them into different classes, actuated by different sentiments and views. The regulation of these various and interfering interests forms the principal task of modern legislation, and involves the spirit of party and faction in the necessary and ordinary operations of government.

No man is allowed to be a judge in his own cause; because his interest will certainly bias his judgment, and, not improbably, corrupt his integrity. With equal, nay, with greater reason, a body of men are unfit to be both judges and parties at the same time; yet what are many of the most important acts of legislation, but so many judicial determinations, not indeed concerning the rights of single persons, but concerning the rights of large bodies of citizens? and what are the different classes of legislators, but advocates and parties to the causes which they determine? Is a law proposed concerning private debts? It is a question to which the creditors are parties on one side, and the debtors on the other. Justice ought to hold the balance between them. Yet the parties are, and must be, themselves the judges: and the most numerous party, or, in other words, the most powerful faction, must be expected to prevail. Shall domestic manufactures be encouraged, and in what degree, by restrictions on foreign manufactures? are questions which would be differently decided by the landed and the manufacturing classes; and probably by neither with a sole regard to justice and the public good. The apportionment of taxes, on the various descriptions of property, is an act which seems to require the most exact impartiality; yet there is, perhaps, no legislative act, in which greater opportunity and temptation are given to a predominant party, to trample on the rules of justice. Every shilling, with which they overburden the inferior number, is a shilling saved to their own pockets.

It is in vain to say, that enlightened statesmen will be able to adjust these clashing interests, and render them all subservient to the public good. Enlightened statesmen will not always be at the helm: nor, in many cases, can such an adjustment be made at all, without taking into view indirect and remote considerations, which will rarely prevail over the immediate interest which one party may find in disregarding the rights of another, or the good of the whole.

The inference to which we are brought is, that the *causes* of faction cannot be removed; and that relief is only to be sought in the means of controlling its *effects*.

If a faction consists of less than a majority, relief is supplied by the republican principle, which enables the majority to defeat its sinister views, by regular vote. It may clog the administration, it may convulse the society; but it will be unable to execute and mask its violence under the forms of the constitution. When a majority is included in a faction, the form of popular government, on the other hand, enables it to sacrifice to its ruling passion or interest, both the public good and the rights of other citizens. To secure the public good, and private rights, against the danger of such a faction, and at the same time to preserve the spirit and the form of popular government, is then the great object to which our inquiries are directed. Let me add, that it is the great desideratum, by which alone this form of government can be rescued from the opprobrium under which it has so long labored, and be recommended to the esteem and adoption of mankind.

By what means is this object attainable? Evidently by one of two only. Either the existence of the same passion or interest in a majority, at the same time must be prevented; or the majority, having such co-existent passion or interest, must be rendered, by their number and local situation, unable to concert and carry into effect schemes of oppression. If the impulse and the opportunity be suffered to coincide, we well know, that neither moral nor religious motives can be relied on as an adequate control. They are not found to be such on the injustice and violence of individuals, and lose their efficacy in proportion to the number combined together; that is, in proportion as their efficacy becomes needful.

From this view of the subject, it may be concluded, that a pure democracy, by which I mean a society consisting of a small number of citizens, who assemble and administer the government in person, can admit of no cure from the mischiefs of faction. A common passion or interest will, in almost every case, be felt by a majority of the whole; a communication and concert, results from the form of government itself; and there is nothing to check the inducements to sacrifice the weaker party, or an obnoxious individual. Hence it is, that such democracies have ever been spectacles of turbulence and contention; have ever been found incompatible with personal security, or the rights of property; and have, in general, been as short in their lives, as they have been violent in their deaths. Theoretic politicians, who have patronized this species of government, have erroneously supposed, that by reducing mankind to a perfect equality in their political rights, they would, at the same time, be perfectly equalized and assimilated in their possessions, their opinions, and their passions.

A republic, by which I mean a government in which the scheme of representation takes place, opens a different prospect, and promises the cure for which we are seeking. Let us examine the points in which it varies from pure democracy, and we shall comprehend both the nature of the cure and the efficacy which it must derive from the union.

The two great points of difference, between a democracy and a republic, are, first, the delegation of the government, in the latter, to a small number of citizens elected by the rest; secondly, the greater number of citizens, and greater sphere of country, over which the latter may be extended.

The effect of the first difference is, on the one hand, to refine and enlarge the public views, by passing them through the medium of a chosen body of citizens, whose wisdom may best discern the true interest of their country, and whose patriotism and love of justice, will be least likely to sacrifice it to temporary or partial considerations. Under such a regulation, it may well happen, that the public voice, pronounced by the representatives of the people, will be more consonant to the public good, than if pronounced by the people themselves, convened for the purpose. On the other hand, the effect may be inverted. Men of factious tempers, of local prejudices, or of sinister designs, may by intrigue, by corruption, or by other means, first obtain the suffrages, and then betray the interests of the people. The question resulting is, whether small or extensive republics are most favorable to the election of proper guardians of the public weal; and it is clearly decided in favor of the latter by two obvious considerations.

In the first place, it is to be remarked, that however small the republic may be, the representatives must be raised to a certain number, in order to guard against the cabals of a few; and that however large it may be, they must be limited to a certain number, in order to guard against the confusion of a multitude. Hence, the number of representatives in the two cases not being in proportion to that of the constituents, and being proportionally greatest in the small republic, it follows that if the proportion of fit characters be not less in the large than in the small republic, the former will present a greater option, and consequently a greater probability of a fit choice.

In the next place, as each representative will be chosen by a greater number of citizens in the large than in the small republic, it will be more difficult for unworthy candidates to practice with success the vicious arts, by which elections are too often carried; and the suffrages of the people being more free, will be more likely to center in men who possess the most attractive merit, and the most diffusive and established characters.

It must be confessed, that in this, as in most other cases, there is a mean, on both sides of which inconveniences will be found to lie. By enlarging too much the number of electors, you render the representative too little acquainted with all their local circumstances and lesser interests; as by reducing it too much, you render him unduly attached to these, and too little fit to comprehend and pursue great and national objects. The federal constitution forms a happy combination in this respect; the great and aggregate interests being referred to the national, the local, and particular to the state legislatures.

The other point of difference is, the greater number of citizens, and extent of territory, which may be brought within the compass of republican, than of democratic government; and it is this circumstance principally which renders factious combinations less to be dreaded in the former, than in the latter. The smaller the society, the fewer probably will be the distinct parties and interests composing it; the fewer the distinct parties and interests, the more frequently will a majority be found of the same party; and the smaller the number of individuals composing a majority, and the smaller the compass within which they are placed, the more easily will they concert and execute their plans of oppression. Extend the sphere, and you take in a greater variety of parties and interests; you make it less probable that a majority of the whole will have a common motive to invade the rights of other citizens; or if such a common motive exists, it will be more difficult for all who feel it to discover their own strength, and to act in unison with each other. Besides other impediments, it may be remarked, that where there is a consciousness of unjust or dishonorable purposes, communication is always checked by distrust, in proportion to the number whose concurrence is necessary.

Hence, it clearly appears, that the same advantage, which a republic has over a democracy, in controlling the effects of faction, is enjoyed by a large over a small republic—is enjoyed by the union over the states composing it. Does this advantage consist in the substitution of representatives, whose enlightened views and virtuous sentiments render them superior to local prejudices, and to schemes of injustice? It will not be denied, that the representation of the union will be most likely to possess these requisite endowments. Does it consist in the greater security afforded by a greater variety of parties, against the event of any one party being able to outnumber and oppress the rest? In an equal degree does the increased variety of parties, comprised within the union, increase this security. Does it, in fine, consist in the greater obstacles opposed to the concert and accomplishment of the secret wishes of an unjust and interested majority? Here, again, the extent of the union gives it the most palpable advantage.

The influence of factious leaders may kindle a flame within their particular states, but will be unable to spread a general conflagration through the other states; a religious sect may degenerate into a political faction in a part of the confederacy; but the variety of sects dispersed over the entire face of it, must secure the national councils against any danger from that source: a rage for paper money, for an abolition of debts, for an equal division of property, or for any other improper or wicked project, will be less apt to pervade the whole body of the union, than a particular member of it; in the same proportion as such a malady is more likely to taint a particular county or district, than an entire state.

In the extent and proper structure of the union, therefore, we behold a republican remedy for the diseases most incident to republican government. And according to the degree of pleasure and pride we feel in being republicans, ought to be our zeal in cherishing the spirit, and supporting the character of federalists.

PUBLIUS.

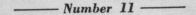

Number 11

Alexander Hamilton

Union and Economic Growth.

The importance of the union, in a commercial light, is one of those points about which there is least room to entertain a difference of opinion, and which has in fact commanded the most general assent of men, who have any acquaintance with the subject. This applies as well to our intercourse with foreign countries, as with each other.

There are appearances to authorize a supposition, that the adventurous spirit, which distinguishes the commercial character of America, has already excited uneasy sensations in several of the maritime powers of Europe. They seem to be apprehensive of our too great interference in that carrying trade, which is the support of their navigation, and the foundation of their naval strength. Those of them, which have colonies in America, look forward, with painful solicitude, to what this country is capable of becoming. They foresee the dangers, that may threaten their American dominions from the neighborhood of states, which have all the dispositions, and would possess all the means, requisite to the creation of a powerful marine. Impressions of this kind will naturally indicate the policy of fostering divisions among us, and of depriving us, as far as possible, of an ACTIVE COMMERCE in our own bottoms. This would answer then the threefold purpose of preventing our interference in their navigation, of monopolizing the profits of our trade, and of clipping the wings, on which we might soar to a dangerous greatness. Did not prudence forbid the detail, it would not be difficult to trace, by facts, the workings of this policy to the cabinets of ministers. If we continue united, we may, in a variety of ways, counteract a policy so unfriendly to our prosperity. By prohibitory regulations, extending at the same time throughout the states, we may oblige foreign countries to bid against each other for the privileges of our markets. This assertion will not appear chimerical to those who are able to appreciate the importance, to any manufacturing nation, of the markets of three millions of people—increasing in rapid progression; for the most part, exclusively addicted to agriculture, and likely from local circumstances to remain in this disposition; and the immense difference there would be to the trade and navigation of such a nation, between a direct communication in its own ships, and an indirect conveyance of its products and returns, to and from America, in the ships of another country. Suppose, for instance, we had a government in America, capable of excluding Great Britain (with whom we have at present no treaty of commerce) from all our ports; what would be the probable operation of this step upon her politics? Would it not enable us to negotiate, with the fairest prospect of success, for commercial privileges of the most valuable and extensive kind, in the dominions of that kingdom? When these questions have been asked, upon other occasions, they have received a plausible, but not a solid or satisfactory answer. It has been said, that prohibitions on our part would produce no change in the system of Britain; because she could prosecute her trade with us, through the medium of the Dutch, who would be her immediate customers and paymasters for those articles which were wanted for the supply of our markets. But would not her navigation be materially injured by the loss of the important advantage of being her own carrier in that trade? Would not the principal part of its profits be intercepted by the Dutch, as a compensation for their agency and risk? Would not the mere circumstance of freight occasion a considerable deduction? Would not so circuitous an intercourse facilitate the competitions of other nations, by enhancing the price of British commodities in our markets, and by transferring to other hands the management of this interesting branch of the British commerce?

A mature consideration of the objects, suggested by these questions, will justify a belief, that the real disadvantages to Great Britain, from such a state of things, conspiring with the prepossessions of a great part of the nation in favor of the American trade, and with the importunities of the West India islands, would produce a relaxation in her present system, and would let us into the enjoyment of privileges in the markets of those islands and elsewhere, from which our trade would derive the most substantial benefits. Such a point gained from the British government, and which could not be expected without an equivalent in exemptions and immunities in our markets, would be likely to have a correspondent effect on the conduct of other nations, who would not be inclined to see themselves altogether supplanted in our trade.

A further resource for influencing the conduct of European nations toward us, in this respect, would arise from the establishment of a federal navy. There can be no doubt, that the continuance of the union, under an efficient government, would put it in our power, at a period not very distant, to create a navy, which, if it should not vie with those of the great maritime powers, would at least be of respectable weight, if thrown into the scale of either of two contending parties. This would be more particularly the case in relation to operations in the West Indies. A few ships of the line, sent opportunely to the reinforcement of either side, would often be sufficient to decide the fate of a campaign, on the event of which, interests of the greatest magnitude were suspended. Our position is, in this respect, a very commanding one. And in to this consideration we add that of the usefulness of supplies from this country, in the prosecution of military operations in the West Indies, it will readily be perceived, that a situation so favorable, would enable us to bargain with great advantage for commercial privileges. A price would be set not only upon our friendship, but upon our neutrality. By a steady adherence to the union, we may hope, ere long, to become the arbiter of Europe in

America; and to be able to incline the balance of European competitions in this part of the world, as our interest may dictate.

But in the reverse of this eligible situation, we shall discover, that the rivalships of the parts would make them checks upon each other, and would frustrate all the tempting advantages which nature has kindly placed within our reach. In a state so insignificant, our commerce would be a prey to the wanton intermeddlings of all nations at war with each other; who, having nothing to fear from us, would, with little scruple or remorse, supply their wants by depredations on our property, as often as it fell in their way. The rights of neutrality will only be respected when they are defended by an adequate power. A nation, despicable by its weakness, forfeits even the privilege of being neutral.

Under a vigorous national government, the natural strength and resources of the country, directed to a common interest, would baffle all the combinations of European jealousy to restrain our growth. This situation would even take away the motive to such combinations, by inducing an impracticability of success. An active commerce, an extensive navigation, a flourishing marine, would then be the inevitable offspring of moral and physical necessity. We might defy the little arts of little politicians to control, or vary, the irresistible and unchangeable course of nature.

But in a state of disunion, these combinations might exist, and might operate with success. It would be in the power of the maritime nations, availing themselves of our universal impotence, to prescribe the conditions of our political existence; and as they have a common interest in being our carriers, and still more in preventing us from becoming theirs, they would, in all probability, combine to embarrass our navigation in such a manner, as would in effect destroy it, and confine us to a PASSIVE COMMERCE. We should thus be compelled to content ourselves with the first price of our commodities, and to see the profits of our trade snatched from us, to enrich our enemies and persecutors. That unequaled spirit of enterprise, which signalizes the genius of the American merchants and navigators, and which is in itself an inexhaustible mine of national wealth, would be stifled and lost; and poverty and disgrace would overspread a country, which, with wisdom, might make herself the admiration and envy of the world.

There are rights of great moment to the trade of America, which are rights of the union: I allude to the fisheries, to the navigation of the Lakes, and to that of the Mississippi. The dissolution of the confederacy would give room for delicate questions, concerning the future existence of these rights; which the interest of more powerful partners would hardly fail to solve to our disadvantage. The disposition of Spain, with regard to the Mississippi, needs no comment. France and Britain are concerned with us in the fisheries; and view them as of the utmost moment to their navigation. They, of course, would hardly remain long indifferent to that decided mastery, of which experience has shown us to be possessed, in this valuable branch of traffic; and by which we are able to under-sell those nations in their own markets. What more natural, than that they should be disposed to exclude from the lists such dangerous competitors?

This branch of trade ought not to be considered as a partial benefit. All the navigating states may in different degrees advantageously participate in it; and under circumstances of a greater extension of mercantile capacity, would not be unlikely to do it. As a nursery of seamen, it now is, or when time shall have more nearly assimilated the principles of navigation in the several states, will become an universal resource. To the establishment of a navy, it must be indispensable.

To this great national object, a NAVY, union will contribute in various ways. Every institution will grow and flourish in proportion to the quantity and extent of the means concentered toward its formation and support. A navy of the United States, as it would embrace the resources of all, is an object far less remote than a navy of any single state, or partial confederacy, which would only embrace the resources of a part. It happens, indeed, that different portions of confederated America, possess each some peculiar advantage for this essential establishment.

The more southern states furnish in greater abundance certain kinds of naval stores—tar, pitch, and turpentine. Their wood, for the construction of ships, is also of a more solid and lasting texture. The difference in the duration of the ships of which the navy might be composed, if chiefly constructed of southern wood, would be of signal importance, either in the view of naval strength, or of national economy. Some of the southern and of the middle states, yield a greater plenty of iron and of better quality. Seamen must chiefly be drawn from the northern hive. The necessity of naval protection to external or maritime commerce, and the conduciveness of that species of commerce, to the prosperity of a navy, are points too manifest to require a particular elucidation. They, by a kind of reaction, mutually beneficial, promote each other.

An unrestrained intercourse between the states themselves, will advance the trade of each, by an interchange of their respective productions, not only for the supply of reciprocal wants, but for exportation to foreign markets. The veins of commerce in every part will be replenished, and will acquire additional motion and vigor from a free circulation of the commodities of every part. Commercial enterprise will have much greater scope, from the diversity in the production of different states. When the staple of one fails, from a bad harvest or unproductive crop, it can call to its aid the staple of another. The variety, not less than the value, of products for exportation, contributes to the activity of foreign commerce. It can be conducted upon much better terms, with a large number of materials of a given value, than with a small number of materials of the same value; arising from the competitions of trade, and from the fluctuations of markets. Particular articles may be in great demand at certain periods, and unsaleable at others; but if there be a variety of articles, it can scarcely happen that they should all be at one time in the latter predicament; and on this account, the operations of the merchant would be less liable to any considerable obstruction or stagnation. The speculative trader will at once perceive the force of these observations; and will acknowledge that the aggregate balance of the commerce of the United States would bid fair to be much more favorable than that of the Thirteen States, without union, or with partial unions.

It may perhaps be replied to this, that whether the states are united or disunited, there would still be an intimate intercourse between them, which would answer the same ends: But this intercourse would be fettered, interrupted, and narrowed, by a multiplicity of causes; which in the course of these papers have been amply detailed. An unity of commercial, as well as political interests, can only result from an unity of government.

There are other points of view, in which this subject might be placed, of a striking and animating kind. But they would lead us too far into the regions of futurity, and would involve topics not proper for newspaper discussion. I shall briefly observe, that our situation invites, and our interests prompt us, to aim at an ascendant in the system of American affairs. The world may politically, as well as geographically, be divided into four parts, each having a distinct set of interests. Unhappily for the other three, Europe, by her arms and by her negotiations; by force and by fraud, has, in different degrees, extended her dominion over them all. Africa, Asia, and America, have successively felt her domination. The superiority she has long maintained, has tempted her to plume herself as the mistress of the world, and to consider the rest of mankind as created for her benefit. Men, admired as profound philosophers, have, in direct terms, attributed to her inhabitants a physical superiority; and have gravely asserted that all animals, and with them the human species, degenerate in America—that even dogs cease to bark, after having breathed awhile in our atmosphere. Facts have too long supported these arrogant pretensions of the European: It belongs to us to vindicate the honor of the human race, and to teach that assuming brother moderation. Union will enable us to do it. Disunion will add another victim to his triumphs. Let Americans disdain to be the instruments of European greatness! Let the Thirteen States, bound together in a strict and indissoluble union, concur in erecting one great American system, superior to the control of all transatlantic force or influence, and able to dictate the terms of the connection between the old and the new world!

Publius.

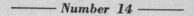

Number 14

James Madison

The Virtues of Bigness.

We have seen the necessity of the union, as our bulwark against foreign danger; as the conservator of peace among ourselves; as the guardian of our commerce, and other common interests; as the only substitute for those military establishments which have subverted the liberties of the old world; and as the proper antidote for the diseases of faction, which have proved fatal to other popular governments, and of which alarming symptoms have been betrayed by our own. All that remains, within this branch of our inquiries, is to take notice of an objection, that may be drawn from the great extent of country which the union embraces. A few observations on this subject will be the more proper, as it is perceived that the adversaries of the new constitution are availing themselves of a prevailing prejudice, with regard to the practicable sphere of republican administration, in order to supply, by imaginary difficulties, the want of those solid objections, which they endeavor in vain to find.

The error which limits republican government to a narrow district, has been unfolded and refuted in preceding papers. I remark here only, that it seems to owe its rise and prevalence chiefly to the confounding of a republic with a democracy; and applying to the former, reasonings drawn from the nature of the latter. The true distinction between these forms, was also adverted to on a former occasion. It is, that in a democracy, the people meet and exercise the government in person: in a republic, they assemble and administer it by their representatives and agents. A democracy, consequently, must be confined to a small spot. A republic may be extended over a large region.

To this accidental source of the error, may be added the artifice of some celebrated authors, whose writings have had a great share in forming the modern standard of political opinions. Being subjects, either of an absolute or limited monarchy, they have endeavored to heighten the advantages, or palliate the evils, of those forms, by placing in comparison with them the vices and defects of the republican, and by citing, as specimens of the latter, the turbulent democracies of ancient Greece and modern Italy. Under the confusion of names, it has been an easy task to transfer to a republic observations applicable to a democracy only; and, among others, the observation, that it can never be established but among a small number of people, living within a small compass of territory.

Such a fallacy may have been the less perceived, as most of the popular governments of antiquity were of the democratic species; and even in modern Europe, to which we owe the great principle of representation, no example is seen of a government wholly popular, and founded, at the same time, wholly on that principle. If Europe has the merit of discovering this great mechanical power in government, by the simple agency of which, the will of the largest political body may be concentered, and its force directed to any object which the public good requires; America can claim the merit of making the discovery the basis of unmixed and extensive republics. It is only to be lamented, that any of her citizens should wish to deprive her of the additional merit of displaying its full efficacy in the establishment of the comprehensive system now under her consideration.

As the natural limit of a democracy is that distance from the central point, which will just permit the most remote citizens to assemble as often as their public functions demand, and will include no greater number than can join in those functions:

so the natural limit of a republic is that distance from the center, which will barely allow the representatives of the people to meet as often as may be necessary for the administration of public affairs. Can it be said that the limits of the United States exceed this distance? It will not be said by those who recollect, that the Atlantic coast is the longest side of the union; that during the term of thirteen years, the representatives of the states have been almost continually assembled; and that the members, from the most distant states, are not chargeable with greater intermissions of attendance, than those from the states in the neighborhood of Congress.

That we may form a juster estimate with regard to this interesting subject, let us resort to the actual dimensions of the union. The limits, as fixed by the treaty of peace, are, on the east the Atlantic, on the south the latitude of thirty-one degrees, on the west the Mississippi, and on the north an irregular line running in some instances beyond the forty-fifth degree, in others falling as low as the forty-second. The southern shore of lake Erie lies below that latitude. Computing the distance between the thirty-first and forty-fifth degrees, it amounts to nine hundred and seventy-three common miles; computing it from thirty-one to forty-two degrees, to seven hundred, sixty-four miles and a half. Taking the mean for the distance, the amount will be eight hundred, sixty-eight miles and three-fourths. The mean distance from the Atlantic to the Mississippi does not probably exceed seven hundred and fifty miles. On a comparison of this extent, with that of several countries in Europe, the practicability of rendering our system commensurate to it, appears to be demonstrable. It is not a great deal larger than Germany, where a diet, representing the whole empire, is continually assembled; or than Poland before the late dismemberment, where another national diet was the depository of the supreme power. Passing by France and Spain, we find that in Great Britain, inferior as it may be in size, the representatives of the northern extremity of the island, have as far to travel to the national council, as will be required of those of the most remote parts of the union.

Favorable as this view of the subject may be, some observations remain, which will place it in a light still more satisfactory.

In the first place, it is to be remembered, that the general government is not to be charged with the whole power of making and administering laws; its jurisdiction is limited to certain enumerated objects, which concern all the members of the republic, but which are not to be attained by the separate provisions of any. The subordinate governments, which can extend their care to all those other objects, which can be separately provided for, will retain their due authority and activity. Were it proposed by the plan of the convention, to abolish the governments of the particular states, its adversaries would have some ground for their objection; though it would not be difficult to show, that if they were abolished, the general government would be compelled, by the principle of self-preservation, to reinstate them in their proper jurisdiction.

A second observation to be made is, that the immediate object of the federal constitution is to secure the union of the thirteen primitive states, which we know to be practicable; and to add to them such other states, as may arise in their own bosoms, or in their neighborhoods, which we cannot doubt to be equally practicable. The arrangements that may be necessary for those angles and fractions of our territory, which lie on our north-western frontier, must be left to those whom further discoveries and experience will render more equal to the task.

Let it be remarked, in the third place, that the intercourse throughout the union will be daily facilitated by new improvements. Roads will everywhere be shortened, and kept in better order; accommodation for travelers will be multiplied and meliorated; an interior navigation on our eastern side, will be opened throughout, or nearly throughout, the whole extent of the Thirteen States. The communication between the western and Atlantic districts, and between different parts of each, will be rendered more and more easy, by those numerous canals, with which the beneficence of nature has intersected our country, and which art finds it so little difficult to connect and complete.

A fourth, and still more important consideration, is, that as almost every state will, on one side or other, be a frontier, and will thus find, in a regard to its safety, an inducement to make some sacrifices for the sake of the general protection: so the states which lie at the greatest distance from the heart of the union, and which of course may partake least of the ordinary circulation of its benefits, will be at the same time immediately contiguous to foreign nations, and will consequently stand, on particular occasions, in greatest need of its strength and resources. It may be inconvenient for Georgia, or the states forming our western or northeastern borders, to send their representatives to the seat of government; but they would find it more so to struggle alone against an invading enemy, or even to support alone the whole expense of those precautions, which may be dictated by the neighborhoods of continual danger. If they should derive less benefit therefore from the union in some respects, than the less distant states, they will derive greater benefit from it in other respects, and thus the proper equilibrium will be maintained throughout.

I submit to you, my fellow-citizens, these considerations, in full confidence that the good sense which has so often marked your decisions, will allow them their due weight and effect; and that you will never suffer difficulties, however formidable in appearance, or however fashionable the error on which they may be founded, to drive you into the gloomy and perilous scenes into which the advocates for disunion would conduct you. Hearken not to the unnatural voice, which tells you that the people of America, knit-together as they are by so many cords of affection, can no longer live together as members of the same family: can no longer continue the mutual guardians of their mutual happiness; can no longer be fellow-citizens of one great, respectable, and flourishing empire. Hearken not to the voice, which petulantly tells you, that the form of government recommended for your adoption, is a novelty in the political world; that it has never yet had a place in the theories of the wildest projectors; that it rashly attempts what it is impossible to accomplish. No, my countrymen, shut your ears against this unhallowed language. Shut your hearts against the poison which it conveys. The kindred blood which flows in the veins of American citizens, the mingled blood which they have shed in defense of their sacred rights, consecrate their union, and excite horror at the idea of their becoming aliens, rivals, enemies. And if novelties are to be shunned, believe me, the most alarming of all novelties, the most wild of all projects, the most rash of all attempts, is that of rending us in pieces, in order to preserve our liberties, and promote our happiness. But why is the experiment of an extended republic to be rejected, merely because it may comprise what is new? Is it not the glory of the people of America, that whilst they have paid a decent regard to the opinions of former times and other nations, they have not suffered a blind veneration for antiquity, for custom, or for names, to overrule the suggestions of their own good sense, the knowledge of their own situation, and the lessons of their own experience? To this manly spirit, posterity will be indebted for the possession, and the world for the example, of the numerous innovations displayed on the American theater, in favor of private rights and public happiness. Had no important step been taken by the leaders of the revolution, for which a precedent could not be discovered; no government established of which an exact model did not present itself, the people of the United States might, at this moment, have been numbered among the melancholy victims of misguided councils; must at best have been laboring under the weight of some of those forms which have crushed the liberties of the rest of mankind. Happily for America, happily, we trust, for the whole human race, they pursued a new and more noble course. They accomplished a revolution which has no parallel in the annals of human society. They reared the fabrics of government which have no model on the face of the globe. They formed the design of a great confederacy, which it is incumbent on their successors to improve and perpetuate. If their works betray imperfections, we wonder at the fewness of them. If they erred most in the structure of the union, this was the work most difficult to be executed; this is the work which has been new modeled by the act of your convention, and it is that act on which you are now to deliberate and to decide.

PUBLIUS.

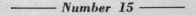

Number 15

Alexander Hamilton

National Law That Will Apply Directly to the Citizens of the States.

In the course of the preceding papers, I have endeavored, my fellow-citizens, to place before you, in a clear and convincing light, the importance of union to your political safety and happiness. I have unfolded to you a complication of dangers to which you would be exposed, should you permit that sacred knot, which binds the people of America together, to be severed or dissolved by ambition or by avarice, by jealousy or by misrepresentation. In the sequel of the inquiry through which I propose to accompany you, the truths intended to be inculcated will receive further confirmation from facts and arguments hitherto unnoticed. If the road, over which you will still have to pass, should in some places appear to you tedious or irksome, you will recollect, that you are in quest of information on a subject the most momentous which can engage the attention of a free people; that the field through which you have to travel is in itself spacious, and that the difficulties of the journey have been unnecessarily increased by the mazes with which sophistry has beset the way. It will be my aim to remove the obstacles to your progress, in as compendious a manner as it can be done without sacrificing utility to dispatch.

In pursuance of the plan, which I have laid down for the discussion of the subject, the point next in order to be examined, is the "insufficiency of the present confederation to the preservation of the union."

It may perhaps be asked, what need there is of reasoning or proof to illustrate a position, which is neither controverted nor doubted; to which the understandings and feelings of all classes of men assent; and which in substance is admitted by the opponents as well as by the friends of the new constitution? It must in truth be acknowledged, that however these may differ in other respects, they in general appear to harmonize in the opinion that there are material imperfections in our national system, and that something is necessary to be done to rescue us from impending anarchy. The facts that support this opinion, are no longer objects of speculation. They have forced themselves upon the sensibility of the people at large, and have at length extorted from those, whose mistaken policy has had the principal share in precipitating the extremity at which we are arrived, a reluctant confession of the reality of many of those defects in the scheme of our federal government, which have been long pointed out and regretted by the intelligent friends of the union.

We may indeed, with propriety, be said to have reached almost the last stage of national humiliation. There is scarcely anything that can wound the pride, or degrade the character, of an independent people, which we do not experience. Are there engagements, to the performance of which we are held by every tie respectable among men? These are the subjects of constant and unblushing violation. Do we owe debts to foreigners, and to our own citizens, contracted in a time of imminent peril, for the preservation of our political existence? These remain without any proper or satisfactory provision for their discharge. Have we valuable territories and important posts in the possession of a foreign power, which, by express stipulations ought long since to have been surrendered? These are still retained, to the prejudice of our interest not less than of our rights. Are we in a condition to resent, or to repel the aggression? We have neither troops, nor treasury, nor government. Are we even in a condition to remonstrate with dignity? The just imputations on our own faith, in respect to the same treaty, ought first to be removed. Are we entitled, by nature and compact, to a free participation in the navigation of the Mississippi? Spain excludes us from it. Is public credit an indispensable resource in time of public danger? We seem to have abandoned its cause as desperate and irretrievable. Is commerce of importance to national wealth? Ours is at the lowest point of declension. Is respectability in the eyes of foreign powers, a safeguard against foreign encroachments? The imbecility of our government even forbids them to treat with us: Our ambassadors abroad are the mere pageants of mimic sovereignty. Is a violent and unnatural decrease in the value of land, a symptom of national distress? The price of improved land, in most parts of the country, is much lower than can be accounted for by the quantity of waste land at market, and can only be fully explained by that want of private and public confidence, which are so alarmingly prevalent among all ranks, and which have a direct tendency to depreciate property of every kind. Is private credit the friend and patron of industry? That most useful kind which relates to borrowing and lending, is reduced within the narrowest limits, and this still more from an opinion of insecurity than from a scarcity of money. To shorten an enumeration of particulars which can afford neither pleasure nor instruction, it may in general be demanded, what indication is there of national disorder, poverty, and insignificance, that could befall a community so peculiarly blessed with natural advantages as we are, which does not form a part of the dark catalogue of our public misfortunes?

This is the melancholy situation to which we have been brought by those very maxims and counsels, which would now deter us from adopting the proposed constitution; and which, not content with having conducted us to the brink of a precipice seem resolved to plunge us into the abyss that awaits us below. Here, my countrymen, impelled by every motive that ought to influence an enlightened people, let us make a firm stand for our safety, our tranquillity, our dignity, our reputation. Let us at last break the fatal charm which has too long seduced us from the paths of felicity and prosperity.

It is true, as has been before observed, that facts too stubborn to be resisted, have produced a species of general assent to the abstract proposition, that there exist material defects in our national system; but the usefulness of the concession, on the part of the old adversaries of federal measures, is destroyed by a strenuous opposition to a remedy, upon the only principles that can give it a chance of success. While they admit that the government of the United States is destitute of energy, they contend against conferring upon it those powers which are requisite to supply that energy. They seem still to aim at things repugnant and irreconcilable; at an augmentation of federal authority, without a diminution of state authority; at sovereignty in the union, and complete independence in the members. They still, in fine, seem to cherish with blind devotion the political monster of an *imperium in imperio*. This renders a full display of the principal defects of the confederation necessary, in order to show, that the evils we experience do not proceed from minute or partial imperfections, but from fundamental errors in the structure of the building, which cannot be amended, otherwise than by an alteration in the very elements and main pillars of the fabric.

The great, and radical vice, in the construction of the existing confederation, is in the principle of LEGISLATION for STATES or GOVERNMENTS, in their CORPORATE or COLLECTIVE CAPACITIES, and as contradistinguished from the INDIVIDUALS of whom they consist. Though this principle does not run through all the powers delegated to the union; yet it pervades and governs those on which the efficacy of the rest depends: Except, as to the rule of apportionment, the United States have an indefinite discretion to make requisitions for men and money; but they have no authority to raise either, by regulations extending to the individual citizens of America. The consequence of this is, that, though in theory, their resolutions concerning those objects, are laws, constitutionally binding on the members of the union, yet, in practice, they are mere recommendations, which the states observe or disregard at their option.

It is a singular instance of the capriciousness of the human mind, that, after all the admonitions we have had from experience on this head, there should still be found men, who object to the new constitution, for deviating from a principle which has been found the bane of the old; and which is, in itself, evidently incompatible with the idea of a GOVERNMENT; a principle, in short, which, if it is to be executed at all, must substitute the violent and sanguinary agency of the sword, to the mild influence of the magistracy.

There is nothing absurd or impracticable, in the idea of a league or alliance between independent nations, for certain defined purposes precisely stated in a treaty; regulating all the details of time, place, circumstance, and quantity; leaving nothing to future discretion; and depending for its execution on the good faith of the parties. Compacts of this kind exist among all civilized nations, subject to the usual vicissitudes of peace and war; of observance and non-observance, as the interests or passions of the contracting powers dictate. In the early part of the present century, there was an epidemical rage in Europe for this species of compacts; from which the politicians of the times fondly hoped for benefits which were never realized. With a view to establishing the equilibrium of power, and the peace of that part of the world, all the resources of negotiation were exhausted, and triple and quadruple alliances were formed; but they were scarcely formed before they were broken, giving an instructive, but afflicting, lesson to mankind, how little dependence is to be placed on treaties which have no other sanction than the obligations of good faith; and which oppose general considerations of peace and justice, to the impulse of any immediate interest of passion.

If the particular states in this country are disposed to stand in a similar relation to each other, and to drop the project of a general DISCRETIONARY SUPERINTENDENCE, the scheme would indeed be pernicious, and would entail upon us all the mischiefs which have been enumerated under the first head; but it would have the merit of being, at least, consistent and practicable. Abandoning all views toward a confederate government, this would bring us to a simple alliance, offensive and defensive; and would place us in a situation to be alternately friends and enemies of each other, as our mutual jealousies and rivalships, nourished by the intrigues of foreign nations, should prescribe to us.

But if we are unwilling to be placed in this perilous situation; if we still adhere to the design of a national government, or, which is the same thing, of a superintending power, under the direction of a common council, we must resolve to incorporate into our plan those ingredients which may be considered as forming the characteristic difference between a league and a government; we must extend the authority of the union to the persons of the citizens—the only proper objects of government.

Government implies the power of making laws. It is essential to the idea of a law, that it be attended with a sanction; or, in other words, a penalty or punishment for disobedience. If there be no penalty annexed to disobedience, the resolutions or commands which pretend to be laws, will in fact amount to nothing more than advice or recommendation. This penalty, whatever it may be, can only be inflicted in two ways; by the agency of the courts and ministers of justice, or by military force; by the COERCION of the magistracy, or by the COERCION of arms. The first kind can evidently apply only to men; the last kind must of necessity be employed against bodies politic, or communities or states. It is evident, that there is no process of a court by which their observance of the laws can, in the last resort, be enforced. Sentences may be denounced against them for violations of their duty; but these sentences can only be carried into execution by the sword. In an association, where the general authority is confined to the collective bodies of the communities that compose it, every breach of the laws must involve a state of war, and military execution must become the only instrument of civil obedience. Such a state of things can certainly not deserve the name of government, nor would any prudent man choose to commit his happiness to it.

There was a time when we were told that breaches, by the

states, of the regulations of the federal authority were not to be expected; that a sense of common interest would preside over the conduct of the respective members, and would beget a full compliance with all the constitutional requisitions of the union. This language, at the present day, would appear as wild as a great part of what we now hear from the same quarter will be thought, when we shall have received further lessons from that best oracle of wisdom, experience. It at all times betrayed an ignorance of the true springs by which human conduct is actuated, and belied the original inducements to the establishment of civil power. Why has government been instituted at all? Because the passions of men will not conform to the dictates of reason and justice, without constraint. Has it been found that bodies of men act with more rectitude or greater disinterestedness than individuals? The contrary of this has been inferred by all accurate observers of the conduct of mankind; and the inference is founded upon obvious reasons. Regard to reputations, has a less active influence, when the infamy of a bad action is to be divided among a number than when it is to fall singly upon one. A spirit of faction, which is apt to mingle its poison in the deliberations of all bodies of men, will often hurry the persons, of whom they are composed, into improprieties and excesses, for which they would blush in a private capacity.

In addition to all this, there is, in the nature of sovereign power, an impatience of control, which disposes those who are invested with the exercise of it, to look with an evil eye upon all external attempts to restrain or direct its operations. From this spirit it happens, that in every political association which is formed upon the principle of uniting in a common interest a number of lesser sovereignties, there will be found a kind of eccentric tendency in the subordinate or inferior orbs, by the operation of which, there will be a perpetual effort in each to fly off from the common center. This tendency is not difficult to be accounted for. It has its origin in the love of power. Power controlled or abridged is almost always the rival and enemy of that power by which it is controlled or abridged. This simple proposition will teach us how little reason there is to expect that the persons entrusted with the administration of the affairs of the particular members of a confederacy, will at all times be ready, with perfect good humor, and an unbiased regard to the public weal, to execute the resolutions or decrees of the general authority. The reverse of this results from the constitution of man.

If therefore the measures of the confederacy cannot be executed, without the intervention of the particular administrations, there will be little prospect of their being executed at all. The rulers of the respective members, whether they have a constitutional right to do it or not, will undertake to judge of the propriety of the measures themselves. They will consider the conformity of the thing proposed or required to their immediate interests or aims; the momentary conveniences or inconveniences that would attend its adoption. All this will be done; and in a spirit of interested and suspicious scrutiny, without that knowledge of national circumstances and reasons of state, which is essential to a right judgment, and with that strong predilection in favor of local objects, which can hardly fail to mislead the decision. The same process must be repeated in every member of which the body is constituted; and the execution of the plans, framed by the councils of the whole, will always fluctuate on the discretion of the ill-informed and prejudiced opinion of every part. Those who have been conversant in the proceedings of popular assemblies; who have seen how difficult it often is, when there is no exterior pressure of circumstances, to bring them to harmonious resolutions on important points, will readily conceive how impossible it must be to induce a number of such assemblies, deliberating at a distance from each other, at different times, and under different impressions, long to co-operate in the same views and pursuits.

In our case, the concurrence of thirteen distinct sovereign wills is requisite under the confederation, to the complete execution of every important measure, that proceeds from the union. It has happened, as was to have been foreseen. The measures of the union have not been executed; the delinquences of the states have, step by step, matured themselves to an extreme, which has at length arrested all the wheels of the national government, and brought them to an awful stand. Congress at this time scarcely possess the means of keeping up the forms of administration, till the states can have time to agree upon a more substantial substitute for the present shadow of a federal government. Things did not come to this desperate extremity at once. The causes which have been specified, produced at first only unequal and disproportionate degrees of compliance with the requisitions of the union. The greater deficiencies of some states furnished the pretext of example, and the temptation of interest to the complying, or at least delinquent states. Why should we do more in proportion than those who are embarked with us in the same political voyage? Why should we consent to bear more than our proper share of the common burden? These were suggestions which human selfishness could not withstand, and which even speculative men, who looked forward to remote consequences, could not without hesitation combat. Each state, yielding to the persuasive voice of immediate interest or convenience, has successively withdrawn its support, till the frail and tottering edifice seems ready to fall upon our heads and to crush us beneath its ruins.

PUBLIUS.

———— *Number 21* ————

Alexander Hamilton

The Enforcement of National Law.

Having taken a summary review of the principal circumstances and events, which depict the genius and fate of other confederate governments, I shall now proceed in the enumeration of the most important of those defects, which have hitherto disappointed our hopes from the system established among ourselves. To form a safe and satisfactory judgment of the proper remedy, it is absolutely necessary that we should be well acquainted with the extent and malignity of the disease.

The next most palpable defect of the existing confederation, is the total want of a SANCTION to its laws. The United States, as now composed, have no power to exact obedience, or punish disobedience to their resolutions, either by pecuniary mulcts, by a suspension or divestiture of privileges, or by any other constitutional means. There is no express delegation of authority to them to use force against delinquent members; and if such a right should be ascribed to the federal head, as resulting from the nature of the social compact between the states, it must be by inference and construction, in the face of that part of the second article, by which it is declared, "that each state shall retain every power, jurisdiction, and right, not *expressly* delegated to the United States in Congress assembled." The want of such a right involves, no doubt, a striking absurdity; but we are reduced to the dilemma, either of supposing that deficiency, preposterous as it may seem, or of contravening or explaining away a provision, which has been of late a repeated theme of the eulogies of those who oppose the new constitution; and the omission of which, in that plan, has been the subject of much plausible animadversion, and severe criticism. If we are unwilling to impair the force of this applauded provision, we shall be obliged to conclude, that the United States afford the extraordinary spectacle of a government, destitute even of the shadow of constitutional power, to enforce the execution of its own laws. It will appear, from the specimens which have been cited, that the American confederacy, in this particular, stands discriminated from every other institution of a similar kind, and exhibits a new and unexampled phenomenon in the political world.

The want of a mutual guarantee of the state governments is another capital imperfection in the federal plan. There is nothing of this kind declared in the articles that compose it: and to imply a tacit guarantee from considerations of utility would be a still more flagrant departure from the clause which has been mentioned, than to imply a tacit power of coercion, from the like considerations. The want of a guarantee, though it might in its consequences endanger the union, does not so immediately attack its existence, as the want of a constitutional sanction to its laws.

Without a guarantee, the assistance to be derived from the union, in repelling those domestic dangers, which may sometimes threaten the existence of the state constitutions, must be renounced. Usurpation may rear its crest in each state, and trample upon the liberties of the people; while the national government could legally do nothing more than behold its encroachments with indignation and regret. A successful faction may erect a tyranny on the ruins of order and law, while no succor could constitutionally be afforded by the union to the friends and supporters of the government. The tempestuous situation, from which Massachusetts has scarcely emerged, evinces, that dangers of this kind are not merely speculative. Who can determine what might have been the issue of her late convulsions, if the malcontents had been headed by a Cæsar or by a Cromwell? Who can predict what effect a despotism, established in Massachusetts, would have upon the liberties of New Hampshire or Rhode Island; of Connecticut or New York?

The inordinate pride of state importance, has suggested to some minds an objection to the principle of a guarantee in the federal government; as involving an officious interference in the domestic concerns of the members. A scruple of this kind would deprive us of one of the principal advantages to be expected from union; and can only flow from a misapprehension of the nature of the provision itself. It could be no impediment to reforms of the state constitutions by a majority of the people in a legal and peaceable mode. This right would remain undiminished. The guarantee could only operate against changes to be effected by violence. Toward the prevention of calamities of this kind, too many checks cannot be provided. The peace of society, and the stability of government, depend absolutely on the efficacy of the precautions adopted on this head. Where the whole power of the government is in the hands of the people, there is the less pretense for the use of violent remedies, in partial or occasional distempers of the state. The natural cure for an ill administration, in a popular or representative constitution, is a change of men. A guarantee by the national authority, would be as much directed against the usurpations of rulers, as against the ferments and outrages of faction and sedition in the community.

The principle of regulating the contributions of the states to the common treasury by QUOTAS, is another fundamental error in the confederation. Its repugnancy to an adequate supply of the national exigencies, has been already pointed out, and has sufficiently appeared from the trial which has been made of it. I speak of it now solely, with a view to equality among the states. Those who have been accustomed to contemplate the circumstances, which produce and constitute national wealth, must be satisfied that there is no common standard, or barometer, by which the degrees of it can be ascertained. Neither the value of lands, nor the numbers of the people, which have been successively proposed as the rule of state contributions, has any pretension to being a just representative. If we compare the wealth of the United Netherlands with that of Russia or Germany, or even of France; and if we at the same time compare the total value of the lands, and the aggregate population of the contracted territory of that republic, with the total value of the lands, and the aggregate population of the immense regions of either of those kingdoms, we shall at once discover that there is no comparison between the proportion of either of these two objects, and that of the relative wealth of those nations. If the like parallel were to be run between several of the American states, it would furnish a like result. Let Virginia be contrasted with North Carolina, Pennsylvania with Connecticut, or Maryland with New Jersey, and we shall be convinced that the respective abilities of those states, in relation to revenue, bear little or no analogy to their comparative stock in lands, or to their comparative population. The position may be equally illustrated, by a similar process between the counties of the same state. No man acquainted with the state of New York will doubt, that the active wealth of King's County bears a much greater proportion to that of Montgomery, than it would appear to do, if we should take either the total value of the lands, or the total numbers of the people as a criterion.

The wealth of nations depends upon an infinite variety of causes. Situation, soil, climate, the nature of the productions, the nature of the government, the genius of the citizens; the degree of information they possess; the state of commerce, of arts, of industry; these circumstances, and many more too complex, minute, or adventitious, to admit of a particular specification, occasion differences hardly conceivable in the relative opulence and riches of different countries. The consequence clearly is, that there can be no common measure of national wealth; and of course, no general or stationary rule, by which the ability of a state to pay taxes can be determined. The attempt, therefore, to regulate the contributions of the members of a confederacy, by any such rule, cannot fail to be productive of glaring inequality, and extreme oppression.

This inequality would of itself be sufficient in America to work the eventual destruction of the union, if any mode of enforcing a compliance with its requisitions could be devised. The suffering states would not long consent to remain associated upon a principle which distributed the public burdens with so unequal a hand; and which was calculated to impoverish and oppress the citizens of some states, while those of others would scarcely be conscious of the small proportion of the weight they were required to sustain. This, however, is an evil inseparable from the principle of quotas and requisitions.

There is no method of steering clear of this inconvenience, but by authorizing the national government to raise its own revenues in its own way. Imposts, excises, and in general all duties upon articles of consumption, may be compared to a fluid, which will in time find its level with the means of paying them. The amount to be contributed by each citizen will in a degree be at his own option, and can be regulated by an attention to his resources. The rich may be extravagant, the poor can be frugal. And private oppression may always be avoided, by a judicious selection of objects proper for such impositions. If inequalities should arise in some states from duties on particular objects, these will, in all probability, be counterbalanced by proportional inequalities in other states, from the duties on other objects. In the course of time and things, an equilibrium, as far as it is attainable, in so complicated a subject, will be established everywhere. Or, if inequalities should still exist, they would neither be so great in their degree, so uniform in their operation, nor so odious in their appearance, as those which would necessarily spring from quotas, upon any scale that can possibly be devised.

It is a signal advantage of taxes on articles of consumption, that they contain in their own nature a security against excess. They prescribe their own limit; which cannot be exceeded without defeating the end proposed—that is, an extension of the revenue. When applied to this object, the saying is as just as it is witty, that "in political arithmetic, two and two do not always make four." If duties are too high, they lessen the consumption—the collection is eluded; and the product to the treasury is not so great as when they are confined within proper and moderate bounds.

This forms a complete barrier against any material oppression of the citizens, by taxes of this class, and is itself a natural limitation of the power of imposing them.

Impositions of this kind fall usually under the denomination of indirect taxes, and must for a long time constitute the chief part of the revenue raised in this country. Those of the direct kind, which principally relate to lands and buildings, may admit of a rule of apportionment. Either the value of land, or the number of the people, may serve as a standard. The state of agriculture, and the populousness of a country, are considered as having a near relation to each other. And as a rule for the purpose intended, numbers in the view of simplicity and certainty, are entitled to a preference. In every country it is an Herculean task to obtain a valuation of the land; in a country imperfectly settled and progressive in improvement, the difficulties are increased almost to impracticability. The expense of an accurate valuation, is in all situations a formidable objection. In a branch of taxation where no limits to the discretion of the government are to be found in the nature of the thing, the establishment of a fixed rule, not incompatible with the end, may be attended with fewer inconveniences than to leave that discretion altogether at large.

PUBLIUS.

------ *Number 23* ------

Alexander Hamilton

Energy in the National Government.

The necessity of a constitution, at least equally energetic with the one proposed, to the preservation of the union, is the point, at the examination of which we are now arrived.

This inquiry will naturally divide itself into three branches. The objects to be provided for by a federal government. The quantity of power necessary to the accomplishment of those objects. The persons upon whom that power ought to operate. Its distribution and organization, will more properly claim our attention under the succeeding head.

The principal purposes to be answered by union, are these: The common defense of the members; the preservation of the public peace, as well against internal convulsions as external attacks; the regulation of commerce with other nations, and between the states; the superintendence of our intercourse, political and commercial, with foreign countries.

The authorities essential to the care of the common defense are these: To raise armies; to build and equip fleets; to prescribe rules for the government of both; to direct their operations; to provide for their support. These powers ought to exist without limitation; because it is impossible to foresee or to define the extent and variety of national exigencies, and the correspondent extent and variety of the means which may be necessary to satisfy them. The circumstances that endanger the safety of nations are infinite; and for this reason, no constitutional shackles can wisely be imposed on the power to which the care of it is committed. This power ought to be co-extensive with all the possible combinations of such circumstances; and ought to be under the direction of the same councils, which are appointed to preside over the common defense.

This is one of those truths, which, to a correct and unprejudiced mind, carries its own evidence along with it; and may be obscured, but cannot be made plainer by argument or reasoning. It rests upon axioms, as simple as they are universal—the *means* ought to be proportioned to the *end;* the persons from whose agency the attainment of any *end* is expected, ought to possess the *means* by which it is to be attained.

Whether there ought to be a federal government entrusted with the care of the common defense, is a question, in the first instance, open to discussion; but the moment it is decided in the affirmative, it will follow, that, that government ought to be clothed with all the powers requisite to the complete execution of its trust. And unless it can be shown, that the circumstances which may affect the public safety, are reducible within certain determinate limits; unless the contrary of this position can be fairly and rationally disputed, it must be admitted as a necessary consequence, that there can be no limitation of that authority, which is to provide for the defense and protection of the community, in any matter essential to its efficacy; that is, in any matter essential to the *formation, direction,* or *support* of the NATIONAL FORCES.

Defective as the present confederation has been proved to be, this principle appears to have been fully recognized by the framers of it; though they have not made proper or adequate provision for its exercise. Congress have an unlimited discretion to make requisitions of men and money; to govern the army and navy; to direct their operations. As their requisitions are made constitutionally binding upon the states, who are in fact under the most solemn obligations to furnish the supplies required of them, the intention evidently was, that the United States should command whatever resources were by them judged requisite to the "common defense and general welfare." It was presumed, that a sense of their true interests, and a regard to the dictates of good faith, would be found sufficient pledges for the punctual performance of the duty of the members to the federal head.

The experiment has, however, demonstrated, that this expectation was ill founded and illusory; and the observations made under the last head will, I imagine, have sufficed to convince the impartial and discerning, that there is an absolute necessity for an entire change in the first principles of the system. That, if we are in earnest about giving the union energy and duration, we must abandon the vain project of legislating upon the states in their collective capacities; we must extend the laws of the federal government to the individual citizens of America; we must discard the fallacious scheme of quotas and requisitions, as equally impracticable and unjust. The result from all this is, that the union ought to be invested with full power to levy troops; to build and equip fleets; and to raise the revenues which will be required for the formation and support of an army and navy, in the customary and ordinary modes practiced in other governments.

If the circumstances of our country are such, as to demand a compound, instead of a simple; a confederate, instead of a sole government; the essential point which will remain to be adjusted, will be to discriminate the OBJECTS, as far as it can be done, which shall appertain to the different provinces or departments of power: allowing to each, the most ample authority for fulfilling THOSE which may be committed to its charge. Shall the union be constituted the guardian of the common safety? Are fleets, and armies, and revenues, necessary to this purpose? The government of the union must be empowered to pass all laws, and to make all regulations which have relation to them. The same must be the case in respect to commerce, and to every other matter to which its jurisdiction is permitted to extend. Is the administration of justice, between the citizens of the same state, the proper department of the local governments? These must possess all the authorities which are connected with this object, and with every other that may be allotted to their particular cognizance and direction. Not to confer in each case a degree of power, commensurate to the end, would be to violate the most obvious rules of prudence and propriety, and improvidently to trust the great interests of the nation to hands which are disabled from managing them with vigor and success.

Who so likely to make suitable provisions for the public defense, as that body to which the guardianship of the public safety is confided? Which, as the center of information, will best understand the extent and urgency of the dangers that threaten; as the representative of the WHOLE, will feel itself most deeply interested in the preservation of every part; which, from the responsibility implied in the duty assigned to it, will be most sensibly impressed with the necessity of proper exertions; and which, by the extension of its authority throughout the states, can alone establish uniformity and concert in the plans and measures, by which the common safety is to be secured? Is there not a manifest inconsistency in devolving upon the federal government the care of the general defense, and leaving in the state governments the *effective* powers, by which it is to be provided for? Is not a want of co-operation the infallible consequence of such a system? And will not weakness, disorder, an undue distribution of the burdens and calamities of war, an unnecessary and intolerable increase of expense, be its natural and inevitable concomitants? Have we not had unequivocal experience of its effects in the course of the revolution, which we have just achieved?

Every view we may take of the subject as candid inquirers after truth, will serve to convince us, that it is both unwise and dangerous to deny the federal government an unconfined authority, in respect to all those objects which are entrusted to its management. It will, indeed, deserve the most vigilant and careful attention of the people, to see that it be modeled in such a manner as to admit of its being safely vested with the requisite powers. If any plan, which has been, or may be, offered to our consideration, should not, upon a dispassionate inspection, be found to answer this description, it ought to be rejected. A government, the constitution of which renders it unfit to be entrusted with all the powers which a free people *ought to delegate to any government,* would be an unsafe and improper depository of the NATIONAL INTEREST. Wherever THESE can with propriety be confided, the coincident powers may safely accompany them. This is the true result of all just reasoning upon the subject. And the adversaries of the plan, promulgated by the convention, would have given a better impression of their candor, if they had confined themselves to showing that the internal structure of the proposed government was such as to render it unworthy of the confidence of the people. They ought not to have wandered into inflammatory declamations and unmeaning cavils, about the extent of the powers. The POWERS are not too extensive for the OBJECTS of federal administration, or, in other words, for the management of our NATIONAL INTERESTS; nor can any satisfactory argument be framed, to show that they are chargeable with such an excess. If it be true, as has been insinuated by some of the writers on the other side, that the difficulty arises from the nature of the thing, and that the extent of the country will not permit us to form a government, in which such ample powers can safely be reposed, it would prove that we ought to contract our views, and resort to the expedient of separate confederacies, which will move within more practicable spheres. For the absurdity must continually stare us in the face, of confiding to a government the direction of the most essential national concerns, without daring to trust it with the authorities which are indispensable to their proper and efficient management. Let us not attempt to reconcile contradictions, but firmly embrace a rational alternative.

I trust, however, that the impracticability of one general system cannot be shown. I am greatly mistaken, if anything of weight has yet been advanced of this tendency; and I flatter myself, that the observations, which have been made in the course of these papers, have served to place the reverse of that position in as clear a light as any matter, still in the womb of time and experience, is susceptible of. This, at all events, must be evident, that the very difficulty itself, drawn from the extent of the country, is the strongest argument in favor of an energetic government; for any other can certainly never preserve the union of so large an empire. If we embrace, as the standard of our political creed, the tenets of those who oppose the adoption of the proposed constitution, we cannot fail to verify the gloomy doctrines, which predict the impracticability of a national system pervading the entire limits of the present confederacy.

PUBLIUS.

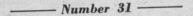

Number 31

Alexander Hamilton

Taxation: The National Taxing Power.

In disquisitions of every kind, there are certain primary truths, or first principles, upon which all subsequent reasonings must depend. These contain an internal evidence, which, antecedent to all reflection or combination, commands the assent of the mind. Where it produces not this effect, it must proceed either from some disorder in the organs of perception, or from the influence of some strong interest, or passion, or prejudice. Of this nature are the maxims in geometry, that the whole is greater than its part; that things equal to the same, are equal to one another; that two straight lines cannot enclose a space, and that all right angles are equal to each other. Of the same nature, are these other maxims in ethics and politics, that there cannot be an effect without a cause; that the means ought to be proportioned to the end; that every power ought to be commensurate with its object; that there ought to be no limitation of a power destined to effect a purpose, which is itself incapable of limitation. And there

are other truths in the two latter sciences, which, if they cannot pretend to rank in the class of axioms, are such direct inferences from them, and so obvious in themselves, and so agreeable to the natural and unsophisticated dictates of common sense, that they challenge the assent of a sound and unbiased mind, with a degree of force and conviction almost equally irresistible.

The objects of geometrical inquiry, are so entirely abstracted from those pursuits which stir up and put in motion the unruly passions of the human heart, that mankind, without difficulty, adopt not only the more simple theorems of the science, but even those abstruse paradoxes which, however they may appear susceptible of demonstration, are at variance with the natural conceptions which the mind, without the aid of philosophy, would be led to entertain upon the subject. The INFINITE DIVISIBILITY of matter, or in other words, the INFINITE divisibility of a FINITE thing, extending even to the minutest atom, is a point agreed among geometricians; though not less incomprehensible to common sense, than any of those mysteries in religion, against which the batteries of infidelity have been so industriously leveled.

But in the sciences of morals and politics, men are found far less tractable. To a certain degree, it is right and useful that this should be the case. Caution and investigation are a necessary armor against error and imposition. But this untractableness may be carried too far, and may degenerate into obstinacy, perverseness, or disingenuity. Though it cannot be pretended, that the principles of moral and political knowledge have, in general, the same degree of certainty with those of the mathematics; yet they have much better claims in this respect, than, to judge from the conduct of men in particular situations, we should be disposed to allow them. The obscurity is much oftener in the passions and prejudices of the reasoner, than in the subject. Men, upon too many occasions, do not give their own understandings fair play; but yielding to some untoward bias, they entangle themselves in words, and confound themselves in subtleties.

How else could it happen (if we admit the objectors to be

sincere in their opposition) that positions so clear as those which manifest the necessity of a general power of taxation in the government of the union, should have to encounter any adversaries among men of discernment? Though these positions have been elsewhere fully stated, they will perhaps not be improperly recapitulated in this place, as introductory to an examination of what may have been offered by way of objection to them. They are in substance as follow:

A government ought to contain in itself every power requisite to the full accomplishment of the objects committed to its care, and to the complete execution of the trusts for which it is responsible; free from every other control, but a regard to the public good and to the sense of the people.

As the duties of superintending the national defense, and of securing the public peace against foreign or domestic violence, involve a provision for casualties and dangers, to which no possible limits can be assigned, the power of making that provision ought to know no other bounds than the exigencies of the nation, and the resources of the community.

As revenue is the essential engine by which the means of answering the national exigencies must be procured, the power of procuring that article in its full extent, must necessarily be comprehended in that of providing for those exigencies.

As theory and practice conspire to prove, that the power of procuring revenue is unavailing, when exercised over the states in their collective capacities, the federal government must of necessity be invested with an unqualified power of taxation in the ordinary modes.

Did not experience evince the contrary, it would be natural to conclude, that the propriety of a general power of taxation in the national government might safely be permitted to rest on the evidence of these propositions, unassisted by any additional arguments or illustrations. But we find, in fact, that the antagonists of the proposed constitution, so far from acquiescing in their justness or truth, seem to make their principal and most zealous effort against this part of the plan. It may therefore be satisfactory to analyze the arguments with which they combat it.

Those of them which have been most labored with that view, seem in substance to amount to this: "It is not true, because the exigencies of the union may not be susceptible of limitation, that its power of laying taxes ought to be unconfined. Revenue is as requisite to the purposes of the local administrations, as to those of the union; and the former are at least of equal importance with the latter, to the happiness of the people. It is therefore as necessary, that the state governments should be able to command the means of supplying their wants, as, that the national government should possess the like faculty, in respect to the wants of the union. But an indefinite power of taxation in the *latter* might, and probably would, in time, deprive the *former* of the means of providing for their own necessities; and would subject them entirely to the mercy of the national legislature. As the laws of the union are to become the supreme law of the land; as it is to have power to pass all laws that may be NECESSARY for carrying into execution, the authorities with which it is proposed to vest it; the national government might at any time abolish the taxes imposed for state objects, upon the pretense of an interference with its own. It might allege a necessity of doing this, in order to give efficacy to the national revenues: And thus all the resources of taxation might, by degrees, become the subjects of federal monopoly, to the entire exclusion and destruction of the state governments."

This mode of reasoning, appears sometimes to turn upon the supposition of usurpation in the national government; at other times, it seems to be designed only as a deduction from the constitutional operation of its intended powers. It is only in the latter light, that it can be admitted to have any pretensions to fairness. The moment we launch into conjectures, about the usurpations of the federal government, we get into an unfathomable abyss, and fairly put ourselves out of the reach of all reasoning. Imagination may range at pleasure, till it gets bewildered amid the labyrinths of an enchanted castle, and knows not on which side to turn to escape from the apparitions which itself has raised. Whatever may be the limits, or modifications, of the powers of the union, it is easy to imagine an endless train of possible dangers; and by indulging an excess of jealousy and timidity, we may bring ourselves to a state of absolute skepticism and irresolution. I repeat here what I have observed in substance in another place, that all observations, founded upon the danger of usurpation, ought to be referred to the composition and structure of the government, not to the nature and extent of its powers. The state governments, by their original constitutions, are invested with complete sovereignty. In what does our security consist against usurpations from that quarter? Doubtless in the manner of their formation, and in a due dependence of those who are to administer them upon the people. If the proposed construction of the federal government be found, upon an impartial examination of it, to be such as to afford, to a proper extent, the same species of security, all apprehensions on the score of usurpation ought to be discarded.

It should not be forgotten, that a disposition in the state governments, to encroach upon the rights of the union, is quite as probable as a disposition in the union to encroach upon the rights of the state governments. What side would be likely to prevail in such a conflict, must depend on the means which the contending parties could employ, toward ensuring success. As in republics, strength is always on the side of the people; and as there are weighty reasons to induce a belief, that the state governments will commonly possess most influence over them, the natural conclusion is, that such contests will be most apt to end to the disadvantage of the union; and that there is greater probability of encroachments by the members upon the federal head, than by the federal head upon the members. But it is evident, that all conjectures of this kind, must be extremely vague and fallible; and that it is by far the safest course to lay them altogether aside; and to confine our attention wholly to the nature and extent of the powers, as they are delineated in the constitution. Everything beyond this, must be left to the prudence and firmness of the people; who, as they will hold the scales in their own hands, it is to be hoped, will always take care to preserve the constitutional equilibrium between the general and the state governments. Upon this ground, which is evidently the true one, it will not be difficult to obviate the objections, which have been made to an indefinite power of taxation in the United States.

PUBLIUS.

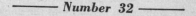

Number 32

Alexander Hamilton

Taxation: The States and the Nation.

Although I am of opinion that there would be no real danger of the consequences to the state governments, which seem to be apprehended from a power in the union to control them in the levies of money; because I am persuaded that the sense of the people, the extreme hazard of provoking the resentments of the state governments, and a conviction of the utility and necessity of local administrations, for local purposes, would be a complete barrier against the oppressive use of such a power: Yet I am willing here to allow, in its full extent, the justness of the reasoning, which requires, that the individual states should possess an independent and uncontrollable authority to raise their own revenues for the supply of their own wants. And making this concession, I affirm that (with the sole exception of duties on imports and exports) they would, under the plan of the convention, retain that authority in the most absolute and unqualified sense; and that an attempt on the part of the national government to abridge them in the exercise of it, would be a violent assumption of power, unwarranted by any article or clause of its constitution.

An entire consolidation of the states into one complete national sovereignty, would imply an entire subordination of the parts; and whatever powers might remain in them, would be altogether dependent on the general will. But as the plan of the convention aims only at a partial union or consolidation, the state governments would clearly retain all the rights of sovereignty which they before had, and which were not, by that act, *exclusively* delegated to the United States. This exclusive delegation, or rather this alienation of state sovereignty, would only exist in three cases; where the constitution in express terms granted an exclusive authority to the union; where it granted, in one instance, an authority to the union; and in another, prohibited the states from exercising the like authority; and where it granted an authority to the union, to which a similar authority in the states would be absolutely and totally *contradictory* and *repugnant*. I use these terms to distinguish this last case from another which might appear to resemble it; but which would, in fact, be essentially different: I mean where the exercise of a concurrent jurisdiction, might be productive of occasional interferences in the *policy* of any branch of administration, but would not imply any direct contradiction or repugnancy in point of constitutional authority. These three cases of exclusive jurisdiction in the federal government, may be exemplified by the following instances: The last clause but one in the eighth section of the first article, provides expressly, that congress shall exercise *"exclusive legislation"* over the district to be appropriated as the seat of government. This answers to the first case. The first clause of the same section empowers congress *"to lay and collect taxes, duties, imposts, and excises";* and the second clause of the tenth section of the same article declares, that *"no state shall,* without the consent of congress, *lay any imposts or duties on imports or exports,* except for the purpose of executing its inspection laws." Hence would result an exclusive power in the union to lay duties on imports and exports, with the particular exception mentioned; but this power is abridged by another clause, which declares, that no tax or duty shall be laid on articles exported from any state; in consequence of which qualification, it now only extends to the *duties on imports*. This answers to the second case. The third will be found in that clause which declares, that congress shall have power "to establish an UNIFORM RULE of naturalization throughout the United States." This must necessarily be exclusive; because if each state had power to prescribe a DISTINCT RULE, there could be no UNIFORM RULE.

A case which may perhaps be thought to resemble the latter, but which is in fact widely different, affects the question immediately under consideration. I mean the power of imposing taxes on all articles other than exports and imports. This, I contend, is manifestly a concurrent and co-equal authority in the United States and in the individual states. There is plainly no expression in the granting clause, which makes that power *exclusive* in the union. There is no independent clause or sentence which prohibits the states from exercising it. So far is this from being the case, that a plain and conclusive argument to the contrary is deducible, from the restraint laid upon the states in relation to duties on imports and exports. This restriction implies an admission, that if it were not inserted, the states would possess the power it excludes, and it implies a further admission, that as to all other taxes, the authority of the states remains undiminished. In any other view it would be both unnecessary and dangerous; it would be unnecessary, because if the grant to the union of the power of laying such duties, implied the exclusion of the states, or even their subordination in this particular, there could be no need of such a restriction; it would be dangerous, because the introduction of it leads directly to the conclusion which has been mentioned, and which, if the reasoning of the objectors be just, could not have been intended; I mean that the states, in all cases to which the restriction did not apply, would have a concurrent power of taxation with the union. The restriction in question amounts to what lawyers call a NEGATIVE PREGNANT; that is, a *negation* of one thing, and an *affirmance* of another; a negation of the authority of the states to impose taxes on imports and exports, and an affirmance of their authority to impose them on all other articles. It would be mere sophistry to argue that it was meant to exclude them *absolutely* from the imposition of taxes of the former kind, and to leave them at liberty to lay others *subject to the control* of the national legislature. The restraining or prohibitory clause only says, that they shall not, *without the consent of congress*, lay such duties; and if we are to understand this is the sense last mentioned, the constitution would then be made to introduce a formal provision, for the sake of a very absurd conclusion; which is, that the states, *with the consent* of the national legislature, might tax imports and exports; and that they might tax every other article, *unless controlled* by the same body. If this was the intention, why was it not left, in the first instance, to what is alleged to be the natural operation of the original clause, conferring a general power of taxation upon the union? It is evident that this could not have been the intention, and that it will not bear a construction of the kind.

As to a supposition of repugnancy between the power of taxation in the states and in the union, it cannot be supported in that sense which would be requisite to work an exclusion of the states. It is indeed possible, that a tax might be laid on a particular article by a state, which might render it *inexpedient* that a further tax should be laid on the same article by the union; but it would not imply a constitutional inability to impose a further tax. The quantity of the imposition, the expediency or inexpediency of an increase on either side, would be mutually questions of prudence; but there would be involved no direct contradiction of power. The particular policy of the national and of the state system of finance, might now and then not exactly coincide, and might require reciprocal forbearances. It is not, however, a mere possibility of inconvenience in the exercise of powers, but an immediate constitutional repugnancy, that can by implication alienate and extinguish a pre-existing right of sovereignty.

The necessity of a concurrent jurisdiction in certain cases, results from the division of the sovereign power; and the rule that all authorities, of which the states are not explicitly divested in favor of the union, remain with them in full vigor, is not only a theoretical consequence of that division but is clearly admitted by the whole tenor of the instrument which contains the articles of the proposed constitution. We there find, that notwithstanding the affirmative grants of general authorities, there has been the most pointed care in those cases where it was deemed improper that the like authorities should reside in the states, to insert negative clauses prohibiting the exercise of them by the states. The tenth section of the first article consists altogether of such provisions. This circumstance is a clear indication of the sense of the convention, and furnishes a rule of interpretation out of the body of the act, which justifies the position I have advanced, and refutes every hypothesis to the contrary.

PUBLIUS.

————— *Number 33* —————

Alexander Hamilton

Taxation: National Supremacy, Necessity and Propriety.

The residue of the argument against the provisions of the constitution, in respect to taxation, is ingrafted upon the following clauses: The last clause of the eighth section of the first article, authorizes the national legislature "to make all laws which shall be *necessary* and *proper*, for carrying into execution *the powers* by that constitution vested in the government of the United States, or in any department or officer thereof"; and the second clause of the sixth article declares, that "the constitution and the laws of the United States made *in pursuance thereof*, and the treaties made by their authority, shall be the *supreme law* of the land; anything in the constitution or laws of any state to the contrary notwithstanding."

These two clauses have been the sources of much virulent invective, and petulant declamation, against the proposed constitution; they have been held up to the people in all the exaggerated colors of misrepresentation, as the pernicious engines by which their local governments were to be destroyed, and their liberties exterminated—as the hideous monster whose devouring jaws would spare neither sex nor age, nor high, nor low, nor sacred, nor profane; and yet, strange as it may appear, after all this clamor, to those who may not have happened to contemplate them in the same light, it may be affirmed with perfect confidence, that the constitutional operation of the intended government would be precisely the same, if these clauses were entirely obliterated, as if they were repeated in every article. They are only declaratory of a truth, which would have resulted by necessary and unavoidable implication from the very act of constituting a federal government, and vesting it with certain specified powers. This is so clear a proposition, that moderation itself can scarcely listen to the railings which have been so copiously vented against this part of the plan, without emotions that disturb its equanimity.

What is a power, but the ability or faculty of doing a thing? What is the ability to do a thing, but the power of employing the *means* necessary to its execution? What is a LEGISLATIVE power, but a power of making LAWS? What are the *means* to execute a LEGISLATIVE power, but LAWS? What is the power of laying and collecting taxes, but a *legislative power*, or a power of *making laws*, to lay and collect taxes? What are the proper means of executing such a power, but *necessary* and *proper* laws?

This simple train of inquiry furnishes us at once with a test of the true nature of the clause complained of. It conducts us to this palpable truth, that a power to lay and collect taxes, must be a power to pass all laws *necessary* and *proper* for the execution of that power: and what does the unfortunate and calumniated provision in question do, more than declare the same truth; to wit, that the national legislature to whom the power of laying and collecting taxes had been previously given, might, in the execution of that power, pass all laws *necessary* and *proper* to carry it into effect? I have applied these observations thus particularly to the power of taxation, because it is the immediate subject under consideration, and because it is the most important of the authorities proposed to be conferred upon the union. But the same process will lead to the same result, in relation to all other powers declared in the constitution. And it is *expressly* to execute these powers, that

the sweeping clause, as it has been affectedly called, authorizes the national legislature to pass all *necessary* and *proper*
laws. If there be anything exceptionable, it must be sought for
in the specific powers, upon which this general declaration is
predicated. The declaration itself, though it may be chargeable with tautology or redundancy, is at least perfectly harm-
less.

But suspicion may ask, why then was it introduced? The answer is, that it could only have been done for greater caution,
and to guard against all caviling refinements in those who
might hereafter feel a disposition to curtail and evade the legitimate authorities of the union. The convention probably
foresaw, what it has been a principal aim of these papers to inculcate, that the danger which most threatens our political welfare, is, that the state governments will finally sap the foundations of the union; and might therefore think it necessary, in so
cardinal a point, to leave nothing to construction. Whatever
may have been the inducement to it, the wisdom of the precaution is evident from the cry which has been raised against
it; as that very cry betrays a disposition to question the great
and essential truth which it is manifestly the object of that
provision to declare.

But it may be again asked, who is to judge of the *necessity*
and *propriety* of the laws to be passed for executing the
powers of the union? I answer, first, that this question arises as
well and as fully upon the simple grant of those powers, as upon the declaratory clause: and I answer, in the second place,
that the national government, like every other, must judge, in
the first instance, of the proper exercise of its powers; and its
constituents in the last. If the federal government should over-
pass the just bounds of its authority, and make a tyrannical
use of its powers; the people, whose creature it is, must appeal
to the standard they have formed, and take such measures to
redress the injury done to the constitution, as the exigency
may suggest and prudence justify. The propriety of a law, in
a constitutional light, must always be determined by the nature of the powers upon which it is founded. Suppose, by
some forced construction of its authority (which indeed can-

not easily be imagined), the federal legislature should attempt to vary the law of descent in any state; would it not be evident, that in making such an attempt, it had exceeded its jurisdiction, and infringed upon that of the state? Suppose, again, that upon the pretense of an interference with its revenues, it should undertake to abrogate a land tax, imposed by the authority of a state; would it not be equally evident, that this was an invasion of that concurrent jurisdiction in respect to this species of tax, which the constitution plainly supposes to exist in the state governments? If there ever should be a doubt on this head, the credit of it will be entirely due to those reasoners, who, in the imprudent zeal of their animosity to the plan of the convention, have labored to envelop it in a cloud, calculated to obscure the plainest and simplest truths.

But it is said, that the laws of the union are to be the *supreme law* of the land. What inference can be drawn from this, or what would they amount to, if they were not to be supreme? It is evident they would amount to nothing. A LAW, by the very meaning of the term, includes supremacy. It is a rule, which those to whom it is prescribed are bound to observe. This results from every political association. If individuals enter into a state of society, the laws of that society must be the supreme regulator of their conduct. If a number of political societies enter into a larger political society, the laws which the latter may enact, pursuant to the powers entrusted to it by its constitution, must necessarily be supreme over those societies, and the individuals of whom they are composed. It would otherwise be a mere treaty, dependent on the good faith of the parties, and not a government; which is only another word for POLITICAL POWER AND SUPREMACY. But it will not follow from this doctrine, that acts of the larger society which are *not pursuant* to its constitutional powers, but which are invasions of the residuary authorities of the smaller societies, will become the supreme law of the land. These will be merely acts of usurpation, and will deserve to be treated as such. Hence we perceive, that the clause which declares the supremacy of the laws of the union, like the one we have just before considered, only declares a truth, which flows immediately and necessarily from the institution of a federal government. It will not, I presume, have escaped observation, that it *expressly* confines this supremacy to laws made *pursuant to the constitution*: which I mention merely as an instance of caution in the convention; since that limitation would have been to be understood, though it had not been expressed.

Though a law, therefore, laying a tax for the use of the United States would be supreme in its nature, and could not legally be opposed or controlled; yet, a law abrogating or preventing the collection of a tax laid by the authority of a state, (unless upon imports and exports) would not be the supreme law of the land, but an usurpation of a power not granted by the constitution. As far as an improper accumulation of taxes, on the same object, might tend to render the collection difficult or precarious, this would be a mutual inconvenience, not arising from a superiority or defect of power on either side, but from an injudicious exercise of power by one or the other, in a manner equally disadvantageous to both. It is to be hoped and presumed, however, that mutual interests would dictate a concert in this respect, which would avoid any material inconvenience. The inference from the whole is—that the individual states would, under the proposed constitution, retain an independent and uncontrollable authority to raise revenue to any extent of which they may stand in need, by every kind of taxation, except duties on imports and exports. It will be shown in the next paper, that this *concurrent jurisdiction* in the article of taxation, was the only admissible substitute for an entire subordination, in respect to this branch of power, of state authority to that of the union.

PUBLIUS.

Alexander Hamilton

Taxation: The Nation and the States.

I flatter myself it has been clearly shown in my last number, that the particular states, under the proposed constitution, would have CO-EQUAL authority with the union in the article of revenue, except as to duties on imports. As this leaves open to the states far the greatest part of the resources of the community, there can be no color for the assertion, that they would not possess means as abundant as could be desired, for the supply of their own wants, independent of all external control. That the field is sufficiently wide, will more fully appear, when we come to develop the inconsiderable share of the public expenses, for which it will fall to the lot of the state governments to provide.

To argue upon abstract principles, that this co-ordinate authority cannot exist, would be to set up theory and supposition against fact and reality. However proper such reasonings might be, to show that a thing *ought not to exist*, they are wholly to be rejected, when they are made use of to prove that it does not exist, contrary to the evidence of the fact itself. It is well known, that in the Roman republic, the legislative authority in the last resort, resided for ages in two different political bodies; not as branches of the same legislature, but as distinct and independent legislatures; in each of which an opposite interest prevailed; in one, the Patrician; in the other, the Plebeian. Many arguments might have been adduced, to prove the unfitness of two such seemingly contradictory authorities, each having power to *annul* or *repeal* the acts of the other. But a man would have been regarded as frantic, who should have attempted at Rome to disprove their existence.

It will readily be understood, that I allude to the COMITIA CENTURIATA and the COMITIA TRIBUTIA. The former, in which the people voted by centuries, was so arranged as to give a superiority to the Patrician interest: In the latter, in which numbers prevailed, the Plebeian interests had an entire predominancy. And yet these two legislatures co-existed for ages, and the Roman republic attained to the pinnacle of human greatness.

In the case particularly under consideration, there is no such contradiction as appears in the example cited; there is no power on either side to annul the acts of the other. And in practice, there is little reason to apprehend any inconvenience; because, in a short course of time, the wants of the states will naturally reduce themselves within *a very narrow compass;* and in the interim, the United States will, in all probability, find it convenient to abstain wholly from those objects to which the particular states would be inclined to resort.

To form a more precise judgment of the true merits of this question, it will be well to advert to the proportion between the objects that will require a federal provision in respect to revenue, and those which will require a state provision. We shall discover that the former are altogether unlimited; and that the latter are circumscribed within very moderate bounds. In pursuing this inquiry, we must bear in mind, that we are not to confine our view to the present period, but to look forward to remote futurity. Constitutions of civil government, are not to be framed upon a calculation of existing exigencies; but upon a combination of these, with the probable exigencies of ages, according to the natural and tried course of human affairs. Nothing, therefore, can be more fallacious, than to infer the extent of any power proper to be lodged in the national government, from an estimate of its immediate necessities. There ought to be a CAPACITY to provide for future contingencies, as they may happen; and as these are illimitable in their nature, so it is impossible safely to limit that capacity. It is true, perhaps, that a computation might be made, with sufficient accuracy to answer the purpose, of the quantity of revenue requisite to discharge the subsisting engagements of the union, and to maintain those establishments, which, for some time to come, would suffice in time of peace. But would it be wise, or would it not rather be the extreme of folly, to stop at this point, and to leave the government entrusted with the care of the national defense, in a state of absolute incapacity to provide for the protection of the community, against future invasions of the public peace, by foreign war or domestic convulsions? If we must be obliged to exceed this point, where can we stop short of an indefinite power of providing for emergencies as they may arise? Though it be easy to assert, in general terms, the possibility of forming a rational judgment of a due provision against probable dangers; yet we may safely challenge those who make the assertion, to bring forward their data, and may affirm, that they would be found as vague and uncertain as any that could be produced to establish the probable duration of the world. Observations, confined to the mere prospects of internal attacks, can deserve no weight; though even these will admit of no satisfactory calculations: But if we mean to be a commercial people, it must form a part of our policy to be able one day to defend that commerce. The support of a navy, and of naval wars, would involve contingencies that must baffle all the efforts of political arithmetic.

Admitting that we ought to try the novel and absurd experiment in politics, of tying up the hands of government from offensive war, founded upon reasons of state: Yet, certainly, we ought not to disable it from guarding the community against the ambition or enmity of other nations. A cloud has been for some time hanging over the European world. If it should break forth into a storm, who can ensure us, that in its progress, a part of its fury would not be spent upon us? No reasonable man would hastily pronounce that we are entirely out of its reach. Or if the combustible materials that now seem to be collecting, should be dissipated without coming to maturity; or if a flame should be kindled without extending to us; what security can we have that our tranquillity will long remain undisturbed from some other cause, or from some other quarter? Let us recollect, that peace or war will not always be left to our option; that however moderate or unambitious we may be, we cannot count upon the moderation, or hope to extinguish the ambition, of others. Who could have imagined, at the conclusion of the last war, that France and Britain, wearied and exhausted as they both were, would already have looked with so hostile an aspect upon each other? To judge from the history of mankind, we shall be compelled to conclude, that the fiery and destructive passions of war, reign in the human breast with much more powerful sway, than the mild and beneficent sentiments of peace; and that to model our political systems upon speculations of lasting tranquillity, would be to calculate on the weaker springs of the human character.

What are the chief sources of expense in every government? What has occasioned that enormous accumulation of debts with which several of the European nations are oppressed? The answer plainly is, wars and rebellions; the support of those institutions which are necessary to guard the body politic against these two most mortal diseases of society. The expenses arising from those institutions which relate to the mere domestic police of a state, to the support of its legislative, executive, and judiciary departments, with their different appendages, and to the encouragement of agriculture and manufactures, (which will comprehend almost all the objects of state expenditure) are insignificant in comparison with those which relate to the national defense.

In the kingdom of Great Britain, where all the ostentatious apparatus of monarchy is to be provided for, not above a fifteenth part of the annual income of the nation is appropriated to the class of expenses last mentioned; the other fourteen-fifteenths are absorbed in the payment of the interests of debts, contracted for carrying on the wars in which that country has been engaged, and in the maintenance of fleets and armies. If, on the one hand, it should be observed, that the expenses incurred in the prosecution of the ambitious enterprises and vainglorious pursuits of a monarchy, are not a proper standard by which to judge of those which might be necessary in a republic; it ought, on the other hand, to be remarked, that there should be as great a disproportion, between the profusion and extravagance of a wealthy kingdom in its domestic administration, and the frugality and economy, which, in that particular, become the modest simplicity of republican government. If we balance a proper deduction from one side, against that which it is supposed ought to be made from the other, the proportion may still be considered as holding good.

But let us take a view of the large debt which we have ourselves contracted in a single war, and let us only calculate on a common share of the events which disturb the peace of nations, and we shall instantly perceive, without the aid of any elaborate illustration, that there must always be an immense disproportion between the objects of federal and state expenditure. It is true, that several of the states, separately, are encumbered with considerable debts, which are an excrescence of the late war. But this cannot happen again, if the proposed system be adopted; and when these debts are discharged, the only call for revenue of any consequence, which the state governments will continue to experience, will be for the mere support of their respective civil lists; to which, if we add all contingencies, the total amount in every state, ought to fall considerably short of a million of dollars.

If it cannot be denied to be a just principle, that in framing a constitution of government for a nation, we ought, in these provisions which are designed to be permanent, to calculate, not on temporary, but on permanent causes of expenses; our attention would be directed to a provision in favor of the state governments, for an annual sum of about 1,000,000 of dollars; while the exigencies of the union could be susceptible of no limits, even in imagination. In this view of the subject, by what logic can it be maintained, that the local governments ought to command, in perpetuity, an *exclusive* source of revenue for any sum beyond that which has been stated? To extend its power further, in *exclusion* of the authority of the union, would be to take the resources of the community out of those hands which stood in need of them for the public welfare, in order to put them into other hands, which could have no just or proper occasion for them.

Suppose, then, the convention had been inclined to proceed upon the principle of a repartition of the objects of revenue, between the union and its members, in *proportion* to their comparative necessities; what particular fund could have been selected for the use of the states, that would not either have been too much or too little; too little for their present, too much for their future wants? As to the line of separation between external and internal taxes, this would leave to the states, at a rough computation, the command of two-thirds of the resources of the community, to defray from a tenth to a twentieth of its expenses; and to the union, one-third of the resources of the community, to defray from nine-tenths to nineteen-twentieths of its expenses. If we desert this boundary, and content ourselves with leaving to the states an exclusive power of taxing houses and lands, there would still be a great disproportion between the *means* and the *end;* the possession of one-third of the resources of the community, to supply, at most, one-tenth of its wants. If any fund could have been selected and appropriated, equal to, and not greater than, the object, it would have been inadequate to the discharge of the existing debts of the particular states, and would have left them dependent on the union for a provision for this purpose.

The preceding train of observations, will justify the position which has been elsewhere laid down, that "A CONCURRENT JURISDICTION in the article of taxation, was the only admissible substitute for an entire subordination, in respect to this branch of power, of state authority to that of the union." Any separation of the objects of revenue that could have been fallen upon, would have amounted to a sacrifice of the great INTERESTS of the union, to the POWER of the individual states. The convention thought the concurrent jurisdiction preferable to that subordination; and it is evident, that it has at least the merit of reconciling an indefinite constitutional power of taxation in the federal government, with an adequate and independent power in the states, to provide for their own necessities. There remain a few other lights, in which this important subject of taxation will claim a further consideration.

PUBLIUS.

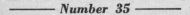 *Number 35*

Alexander Hamilton

Taxation: The Role of the House of Representatives.

Before we proceed to examine any other objections to an indefinite power of taxation in the union, I shall make one general remark; which is, that if the jurisdiction of the national government, in the article of revenue, should be restricted to particular objects, it would naturally occasion an undue proportion of the public burdens to fall upon those objects. Two evils would spring from this source—the oppression of particular branches of industry, and an unequal distribution of the taxes, as well among the several states, as among the citizens of the same state.

Suppose, as has been contended for, the federal power of taxation were to be confined to duties on imports; it is evident that the government, for want of being able to command other resources, would frequently be tempted to extend these duties to an injurious excess. There are persons who imagine that this can never be the case; since the higher they are, the more it is alleged they will tend to discourage an extravagant consumption, to produce a favorable balance of trade, and to promote domestic manufactures. But all extremes are pernicious in various ways. Exorbitant duties on imported articles, serve to beget a general spirit of smuggling; which is always prejudicial to the fair trader, and eventually to the revenue itself:

They tend to render other classes of the community tributary, in an improper degree, to the manufacturing classes, to whom they give a premature monopoly of the markets: They sometimes force industry out of its most natural channels into others, in which it flows with less advantage. And in the last place, they oppress the merchant, who is often obliged to pay them himself, without any retribution from the consumer. When the demand is equal to the quantity of goods at market, the consumer generally pays the duty; but when the markets happen to be overstocked, a great proportion falls upon the merchant, and sometimes not only exhausts his profits, but breaks in upon his capital. I am apt to think, that a division of the duty, between the seller and the buyer, more often happens than is commonly imagined. It is not always possible to raise the price of a commodity, in exact proportion to every additional imposition laid upon it. The merchant, especially in a country of small commercial capital, is often under a necessity of keeping prices down, in order to a more expeditious sale.

The maxim, that the consumer is the payer, is so much oftener true than the reverse of the proposition, that it is far more equitable that the duties on imports should go into a common stock, than that they should redound to the exclusive benefit of the importing states. But it is not so generally true, as to render it equitable, that those duties should form the only national fund. When they are paid by the merchant, they operate as an additional tax upon the importing state; whose citizens pay their proportion of them in the character of consumers. In this view, they are productive of inequality among the states; which inequality would be increased with the increased extent of the duties. The confinement of the national revenues to this species of imposts, would be attended with inequality, from a different cause, between the manufacturing and the non-manufacturing states. The states which can go furthest toward the supply of their own wants, by their own manufactures, will not, according to their numbers or wealth, consume so great a proportion of imported articles, as those states which are not in the same favorable situation; they would not, therefore, in this mode alone, contribute to the public treasury in a ratio to their abilities. To make them do this, it is necessary that recourse be had to excises; the proper objects of which are particular kinds of manufactures. New York is more deeply interested in these considerations, than such of her citizens, as contend for limiting the power of the union to external taxation, may be aware of. New York is an importing state, and from a greater disproportion between her population and territory, is less likely, than some other states, speedily to become in any considerable degree a manufacturing state. She would, of course, suffer, in a double light, from restraining the jurisdiction of the union to commercial imposts.

So far as these observations tend to inculcate a danger of the import duties being extended to an injurious extreme, it may be observed, conformably to a remark made in another part of these papers, that the interest of the revenue itself would be a sufficient guard against such an extreme. I readily admit that this would be the case, as long as other resources were open; but if the avenues to them were closed, HOPE, stimulated by necessity, might beget experiments, fortified by rigorous precautions and additional penalties; which, for a time, might have the intended effect, till there had been leisure to contrive expedients to elude these new precautions. The first success would be apt to inspire false opinions; which it might require a long course of subsequent experience to correct. Necessity, especially in politics, often occasions false hopes, false reasonings, and a system of measures correspondently erroneous. But even if this supposed excess should not be a consequence of the limitation of the federal power of taxation, the inequalities spoken of would still ensue, though not in the same degree, from the other causes that have been noticed. Let us now return to the examination of objections.

One which, if we may judge from the frequency of its repetition, seems most to be relied on, is, that the house of representatives is not sufficiently numerous for the reception of all the different classes of citizens; in order to combine the interests and feelings of every part of the community, and to produce a due sympathy between the representative body and its constituents. This argument presents itself under a very specious and seducing form; and is well calculated to lay hold of the prejudices of those to whom it is addressed. But when we come to dissect it with attention, it will appear to be made up of nothing but fair sounding words. The object it seems to aim at, is in the first place impracticable, and in the sense in which it is contended for, is unnecessary. I reserve for another place, the discussion of the question which relates to the sufficiency of the representative body in respect to numbers; and shall content myself with examining here the particular use which has been made of a contrary supposition, in reference to the immediate subject of our inquiries.

The idea of an actual representation of all classes of the people, by persons of each class, is altogether visionary. Unless it were expressly provided in the constitution, that each different occupation should send one or more members, the thing would never take place in practice. Mechanics and manufacturers will always be inclined, with few exceptions, to give their votes to merchants, in preference to persons of their own professions or trades. Those discerning citizens are well aware, that the mechanic and manufacturing arts furnish the materials of mercantile enterprise and industry. Many of them, indeed, are immediately connected with the operations of commerce. They know that the merchant is their natural patron and friend; and they are aware, that however great the confidence they may justly feel in their own good sense, their interests can be more effectually promoted by the merchant than by themselves. They are sensible that their habits of life have not been such as to give them those acquired endowments, without which, in a deliberative assembly, the greatest natural abilities are for the most part useless; and that the influence and weight and superior acquirements of the merchants, render them more equal to a contest with any spirit which might happen to infuse itself into the public councils, unfriendly to the manufacturing and trading interests. These considerations, and many others that might be mentioned, prove, and experience confirms it, that artisans and manufacturers, will commonly be disposed to bestow their votes upon merchants and those whom they recommend. We must therefore consider merchants as the natural representatives of all these classes of the community.

With regard to the learned professions, little need be observed; they truly form no distinct interest in society; and according to their situation and talents, will be indiscriminately the objects of the confidence and choice of each other, and of other parts of the community.

Nothing remains but the landed interest; and this, in a political view, and particularly in relation to taxes, I take to be perfectly united, from the wealthiest landlord, down to the poorest tenant. No tax can be laid on land which will not affect the proprietor of thousands of acres, as well as the proprietor of a single acre. Every landholder will therefore have a common interest to keep the taxes on land as low as possible; and common interest may always be reckoned upon as the surest bond of sympathy. But if we even could suppose a distinction of interests between the opulent landholder, and the middling farmer, what reason is there to conclude, that the first would stand a better chance of being deputed to the national legislature than the last? If we take fact as our guide, and look into our own senate and assembly, we shall find that moderate proprietors of land prevail in both; nor is this less the case in the senate, which consists of a smaller number than in the assembly, which is composed of a greater number. Where the qualifications of the electors are the same, whether they have to choose a small or large number, their votes will fall upon those in whom they have most confidence; whether these happen to be men of large fortunes, or of moderate property, or of no property at all.

It is said to be necessary that all classes of citizens should have some of their own number in the representative body, in order that their feelings and interests may be the better understood and attended to. But we have seen that this will never happen under any arrangement that leaves the votes of the people free. Where this is the case, the representative body, with too few exceptions to have any influence on the spirit of the government, will be composed of landholders, merchants, and men of the learned professions. But where is the danger that the interests and feelings of the different classes of citizens will not be understood, or attended to by these three descriptions of men? Will not the landholder know and feel whatever will promote or injure the interests of landed property? and will he not, from his own interest in that species of property, be sufficiently prone to resist every attempt to prejudice or encumber it? Will not the merchant understand and be disposed to cultivate, as far as may be proper, the interests of the mechanic and manufacturing arts, to which his commerce is so nearly allied? Will not the man of the learned profession, who will feel a neutrality to the rivalships among the different branches of industry, be likely to prove an impartial arbiter between them, ready to promote either, so far as it shall appear to him conducive to the general interests of the community?

If we take into the account the momentary humors or dispositions which may happen to prevail in particular parts of the society, and to which a wise administration will never be inattentive, is the man whose situation leads to extensive inquiry and information less likely to be a competent judge of their nature, extent, and foundation, than one whose observation does not travel beyond the circle of his neighbors and acquaintances? Is it not natural that a man who is a candidate for the favor of the people, and who is dependent on the suffrages of his fellow citizens for the continuance of his public honors, should take care to inform himself of their dispositions and inclinations, and should be willing to allow them their proper degree of influence upon his conduct? This dependence, and the necessity of being bound himself and his posterity, by the laws to which he gives his assent, are the true, and they are the strong cords of sympathy between the representative and the constituent.

There is no part of the administration of government that requires extensive information, and a thorough knowledge of the principles of political economy, so much as the business of taxation. The man who understands those principles best, will be least likely to resort to oppressive expedients, or to sacrifice any particular class of citizens to the procurement of revenue. It might be demonstrated that the most productive system of finance will always be the least burdensome. There can be no doubt that, in order to a judicious exercise of the power of taxation, it is necessary that the person in whose hands it is, should be acquainted with the general genius, habits, and modes of thinking, of the people at large, and with the resources of the country. And this is all that can be reasonably meant by a knowledge of the interests and feelings of the people. In any other sense, the proposition has either no meaning, or an absurd one. And in that sense, let every considerate citizen judge for himself, where the requisite qualification is most likely to be found.

PUBLIUS.

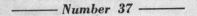

--------- *Number 37* ---------

James Madison

The Dilemmas of the Constitutional Convention.

In reviewing the defects of the existing confederation, and showing that they cannot be supplied by a government of less energy than that before the public, several of the most important principles of the latter fell, of course, under consideration. But as the ultimate object of these papers is, to determine clearly and fully the merits of this constitution, and the expediency of adopting it, our plan cannot be completed without taking a more critical and thorough survey of the work of the convention; without examining it on all its sides; comparing it in all its parts, and calculating its probable effects.

That this remaining task may be executed under impressions conducive to a just and fair result, some reflections must in this place be indulged, which candor previously suggests.

It is a misfortune, inseparable from human affairs, that public measures are rarely investigated with that spirit of moderation, which is essential to a just estimate of their real tendency to advance, or obstruct, the public good; and that this spirit is more apt to be diminished than promoted, by those occasions which require an unusual exercise of it. To those who have been led by experience to attend to this consideration, it could not appear surprising, that the act of the convention which recommends so many important changes and innovations, which may be viewed in so many lights and relations, and which touches the springs of so many passions and interests, should find or excite dispositions unfriendly, both on one side and on the other, to a fair discussion and accurate judgment of its merits. In some, it has been too evident from their own publications, that they have scanned the proposed constitution, not only with a predisposition to censure, but with a predetermination to condemn; as the language held by others, betrays an opposite predetermination or bias, which must render their opinions also of little moment in the question. In placing, however, these different characters on a level, with respect to the weight of their opinions, I wish not to insinuate that there may not be a material difference in the purity of their intentions. It is but just to remark in favor of the latter description, that as our situation is universally admitted to be peculiarly critical, and to require indispensably, that something should be done for our relief, the predetermined patron of what has been actually done, may have taken his bias from the weight of these considerations, as well as from considerations of a sinister nature. The predetermined adversary, on the other hand, can have been governed by no venial motive whatever. The intentions of the first may be upright, as they may on the contrary be culpable. The views of the last cannot be upright, and must be culpable. But the truth is, that these papers are not addressed to persons falling under either of these characters. They solicit the attention of those only, who add to a sincere zeal for the happiness of their country, a temper favorable to a just estimate of the means of promoting it.

Persons of this character will proceed to an examination of the plan submitted by the convention, not only without a disposition to find or to magnify faults; but will see the propriety of reflecting, that a faultless plan was not to be expected. Nor will they barely make allowances for the errors which may be chargeable on the fallibility to which the convention, as a body of men, were liable, but will keep in mind, that they themselves also are but men, and ought not to assume an infallibility in prejudging the fallible opinions of others.

With equal readiness will it be perceived, that besides these inducements to candor, many allowances ought to be made for the difficulties inherent in the very nature of the undertaking referred to the convention.

The novelty of the undertaking immediately strikes us. It has been shown in the course of these papers, that the existing confederation is founded on principles which are fallacious; that we must consequently change this foundation, and with it the superstructure resting upon it. It has been shown, that the other confederacies which could be consulted as precedents, have been vitiated by the same erroneous principles, and can therefore furnish no other light than that of beacons, which give warning of the course to be shunned, without pointing out that which ought to be pursued. The most that the convention could do in such a situation, was to avoid the errors suggested by the past experience of other countries, as well as of our own; and to provide a convenient mode of rectifying their own errors as future experience may unfold them.

Among the difficulties encountered by the convention, a very important one must have lain, in combining the requisite stability and energy in government, with the inviolable attention due to liberty, and to the republican form. Without substantially accomplishing this part of their undertaking, they would have very imperfectly fulfilled the object of their appointment, or the expectation of the public; yet that it could not be easily accomplished, will be denied by no one who is unwilling to betray his ignorance of the subject. Energy in government is essential to that security against external and internal dangers, and to that prompt and salutary execution of the laws, which enter into the very definition of good government. Stability in government is essential to national character, and to the advantages annexed to it, as well as to that repose and confidence in the minds of the people, which are among the chief blessings of civil society. An irregular and mutable legislation is not more an evil in itself, than it is odious to the people; and it may be pronounced with assurance, that the people of this country, enlightened as they are, with regard to the nature, and interested, as the great body of them are, in the effects of good government, will never be satisfied, till some remedy be applied to the vicissitudes and uncertainties, which characterize the state administrations. On comparing, however, these valuable ingredients with the vital principles of liberty, we must perceive at once the difficulty of mingling them together in their due proportions. The genius of republican liberty seems to demand on one side, not only that all power should be derived from the people; but that those entrusted with it should be kept in dependence on the people, by a short duration of their appointments; and that even during this short period, the trust should be placed not in a few, but in a number of hands. Stability, on the contrary, requires, that the hands, in which power is lodged, should continue for a length of time the same. A frequent change of men will result from a frequent return of elections; and a frequent change of measures, from a frequent change of men: whilst energy of government requires not only a certain duration of power, but the execution of it by a single hand.

How far the convention may have succeeded in this part of their work, will better appear on a more accurate view of it. From the cursory view here taken, it must clearly appear to have been an arduous part.

Not less arduous must have been the task of marking the proper line of partition, between the authority of the general, and that of the state governments. Every man will be sensible of this difficulty, in proportion as he has been accustomed to contemplate and discriminate objects, extensive and complicated in their nature. The faculties of the mind itself have never yet been distinguished and defined, with satisfactory precision, by all the efforts of the most acute and metaphysical philosophers. Sense, perception, judgment, desire, volition, memory, imagination, are found to be separated, by such delicate shades and minute gradations, that their boundaries have eluded the most subtle investigations, and remain a pregnant source of ingenious disquisition and controversy. The boundaries between the great kingdoms of nature, and, still more, between the various provinces, and lesser portions, into which they are subdivided, afford another illustration of the same important truth. The most sagacious and laborious naturalists have never yet succeeded, in tracing with certainty the line which separates the district of vegetable life, from the neighboring region of unorganized matter, or which marks the termination of the former, and the commencement of the animal empire. A still greater obscurity lies in the distinctive characters, by which the objects in each of these great departments of nature have been arranged and assorted.

When we pass from the works of nature, in which all the delineations are perfectly accurate, and appear to be otherwise only from the imperfection of the eye which surveys them, to the institutions of man, in which the obscurity arises as well from the object itself, as from the organ by which it is contemplated; we must perceive the necessity of moderating still further our expectations and hopes from the efforts of human sagacity. Experience has instructed us, that no skill in the science of government has yet been able to discriminate and define, with sufficient certainty, its three great provinces, the legislative, executive, and judiciary; or even the privileges and powers of the different legislative branches. Questions daily occur in the course of practice, which prove the obscurity which reigns in these subjects, and which puzzle the greatest adepts in political science.

The experience of ages, with the continued and combined labors of the most enlightened legislators and jurists, have been equally unsuccessful in delineating the several objects and limits of different codes of laws, and different tribunals of justice. The precise extent of the common law, the statute law, the maritime law, the ecclesiastical law, the law of corporations, and other local laws and customs, remain still to be clearly and finally established in Great Britain, where accuracy in such subjects has been more industriously pursued than in any other part of the world. The jurisdiction of her several courts, general and local of law, of equity, of admiralty, etc., is not less a source of frequent and intricate discussions, sufficiently denoting the indeterminate limits by which they are respectively circumscribed. All new laws, though penned with the greatest technical skill, and passed on the fullest and most mature deliberation, are considered as more or less obscure and equivocal, until their meaning be liquidated and ascertained by a series of particular discussions and adjudications. Besides the obscurity arising from the complexity of objects, and the imperfection of the human faculties, the medium through which the conceptions of men are conveyed to each other, adds a fresh embarrassment. The use of words is to express ideas. Perspicuity therefore requires, not only that the ideas should be distinctly formed, but that they should be expressed by words distinctly and exclusively appropriated to them. But no language is so copious as to supply words and phrases for every complex idea, or so correct as not to include many, equivocally denoting different ideas. Hence it must happen, that however accurately objects may be discriminated in themselves, and however accurately the discrimination may be conceived, the definition of them may be rendered inaccurate, by the inaccuracy of the terms in which it is delivered. And this unavoidable inaccuracy must be greater or less, according to the complexity and novelty of the objects defined. When the Almighty himself condescends to address mankind in their own language, his meaning, luminous as it must be, is rendered dim and doubtful, by the cloudy medium through which it is communicated.

Here, then, are three sources of vague and incorrect definitions; indistinctness of the object, imperfection of the organ of perception, inadequateness of the vehicle if ideas. Any one of these must produce a certain degree of obscurity. The convention, in delineating the boundary between the federal and state jurisdictions, must have experienced the full effect of them all.

To the difficulties already mentioned, may be added the interfering pretensions of the larger and smaller states. We cannot err, in supposing that the former would contend for a participation in the government, fully proportioned to their superior wealth and importance; and that the latter would not be less tenacious of the equality at present enjoyed by them. We may well suppose, that neither side would entirely yield to the other, and consequently that the struggle could be terminated only by compromise. It is extremely probable also, that after the ratio of representation had been adjusted, this very compromise must have produced a fresh struggle between the same parties, to give such a turn to the organization of the government, and to the distribution of its powers, as would increase the importance of the branches, in forming which they had respectively obtained the greatest share of influence. There are features in the constitution which warrant each of these suppositions; and as far as either of them is well founded, it shows that the convention must have been compelled to sacrifice theoretical propriety, to the force of extraneous considerations.

Nor could it have been the large and small states only, which would marshal themselves in opposition to each other on various points. Other combinations, resulting from a difference of local position and policy, must have created additional difficulties. As every state may be divided into different districts, and its citizens into different classes, which give birth to contending interests and local jealousies; so the different parts of the United States are distinguished from each other, by a variety of circumstances, which produce a like effect on a larger scale. And although this variety of interests, for reasons sufficiently explained in a former paper, may have a salutary influence on the administration of the government, when formed; yet every one must be sensible of the contrary influence, which must have been experienced in the task of forming it.

Would it be wonderful, if under the pressure of all these difficulties, the convention should have been forced into some deviations from that artificial structure and regular symmetry, which an abstract view of the subject might lead an ingenious theorist to bestow on a constitution planned in his closet, or in his imagination? The real wonder is that so many difficulties should have been surmounted; and surmounted with an unanimity almost as unprecedented, as it must have been unexpected. It is impossible for any man of candor to reflect on this circumstance, without partaking of the astonishment. It is impossible, for the man of pious reflection, not to perceive in it a finger of that Almighty Hand, which has been so frequently and signally extended to our relief in the critical stages of the revolution.

We had occasion, in a former paper, to take notice of the repeated trials which have been unsuccessfully made in the United Netherlands, for reforming the baneful and notorious vices of their constitution. The history of almost all the great councils and consultations, held among mankind for reconciling their discordant opinions, assuaging their mutual jealousies, and adjusting their respective interests, is a history of factions, contentions, and disappointments; and may be classed among the most dark and degrading pictures, which display the infirmities and depravities of the human character. If, in a few scattered instances, a brighter aspect is presented, they serve only as exceptions to admonish us of the general truth; and by their luster to darken the gloom of the adverse prospect, to which they are contrasted. In revolving the causes from which these exceptions result, and applying them to the particular instance before us, we are necessarily led to two important conclusions. The first is, that the convention must have enjoyed, in a very singular degree, an exemption from the pestilential influence of party animosities—the disease most incident to deliberative bodies and most apt to contaminate their proceedings. The second conclusion is that all the deputations composing the convention were satisfactorily accommodated by the final act, or were induced to accede to it by a deep conviction of the necessity of sacrificing private opinions and partial interests to the public good, and by a despair of seeing this necessity diminished by delays or by new experiments.

PUBLIUS.

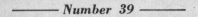

Number 39

James Madison

Republicanism and Federalism.

The last paper having concluded the observations, which were meant to introduce a candid survey of the plan of government reported by the convention, we now proceed to the execution of that part of our undertaking.

The first question that offers itself is, whether the general form and aspect of the government be strictly republican? It is evident that no other form would be reconcilable with the genius of the people of America; with the fundamental principles of the revolution; or with that honorable determination which animates every votary of freedom, to rest all our political experiments on the capacity of mankind for self-government. If the plan of the convention, therefore, be found to depart from the republican character, its advocates must abandon it as no longer defensible.

What, then, are the distinctive characters of the republican form? Were an answer to this question to be sought, not by recurring to principles, but in the application of the term by political writers, to the constitutions of different states, no satisfactory one would ever be found. Holland, in which no particle of the supreme authority is derived from the people, has passed almost universally under the denomination of a republic. The same title has been bestowed on Venice, where absolute power over the great body of the people is exercised, in the most absolute manner, by a small body of hereditary nobles. Poland, which is a mixture of aristocracy and of monarchy in their worst forms, has been dignified with the same appellation. The government of England, which has one republican branch only, combined with a hereditary aristocracy and monarchy, has, with equal impropriety, been frequently placed on the list of republics. These examples, which are nearly as dissimilar to each other as to a genuine republic, show the extreme inaccuracy with which the term has been used in political disquisitions.

If we resort, for a criterion, to the different principles on which different forms of government are established, we may define a republic to be, or at least may bestow that name on, a government which derives all its powers directly or indirectly from the great body of the people, and is administered by persons holding their offices during pleasure, for a limited period, or during good behavior. It is *essential* to such a government, that it be derived from the great body of the society, not from an inconsiderable proportion, or a favored class of it; otherwise a handful of tyrannical nobles, exercising their oppressions by a delegation of their powers, might aspire to the rank of republicans, and claim for their government the honorable title of republic. It is *sufficient* for such a government, that the persons administering it be appointed, either directly or indirectly, by the people; and that they hold their appointments by either of the tenures just specified; otherwise every government in the United States, as well as every other popular government that has been or can be well organized or well executed, would be degraded from the republican character. According to the constitution of every state in the union, some or other of the officers of government are appointed indirectly only by the people. According to most of them, the chief magistrate himself is so appointed. And according to one, this mode of appointment is extended to one of the co-ordinate branches of the legislature. According to all the constitutions also, the tenure of the highest offices is extended to a definite period, and in many instances, both within the legislative and executive departments, to a period of years. According to the provisions of most of the constitutions, again, as well as according to the most respectable and received opinions on the subject, the members of the judiciary department are to retain their offices by the firm tenure of good behavior.

On comparing the constitution planned by the convention, with the standard here fixed, we perceive at once, that it is, in the most rigid sense, conformable to it. The house of representatives, like that of one branch at least of all the state legislatures, is elected immediately by the great body of the people. The senate, like the present congress, and the senate of Maryland, derives its appointment indirectly from the people. The president is indirectly derived from the choice of the people, according to the example in most of the states. Even the judges, with all other officers of the union, will, as in the several states, be the choice, though a remote choice, of the people themselves. The duration of the appointments is equally conformable to the republican standard, and to the model of the state constitutions. The house of representatives is periodically elective, as in all the states; and for the period of two years, as in the state of South Carolina. The senate is elective, for the period of six years; which is but one year more than the period of the senate of Maryland; and but two more than that of the senates of New York and Virginia. The president is to continue in office for the period of four years; as in New York and Delaware, the chief magistrate is elected for three years, and in South Carolina for two years. In the other states the election is annual. In several of the states, however, no explicit provision is made for the impeachment of the chief magistrate. And in Delaware and Virginia, he is not impeachable till out of office. The president of the United States is impeachable at any time during his continuance in office. The tenure by which the judges are to hold their places, is, as it unquestionably ought to be, that of good behavior. The tenure of the ministerial offices generally, will be a subject of legal regulation, conformably to the reason of the case, and the example of the state constitutions.

Could any further proof be required of the republican complexion of this system, the most decisive one might be found in its absolute prohibition of titles of nobility, both under the federal and the state governments; and in its express guarantee of the republican form to each of the latter.

But it was not sufficient, say the adversaries of the proposed constitution, for the convention to adhere to the republican form. They ought, with equal care, to have preserved the *federal* form, which regards the union as a *confederacy* of sovereign states; instead of which, they have framed a *national* government, which regards the union as a *consolidation* of the states. And it is asked, by what authority this bold and radical innovation was undertaken? The handle which has been made of this objection requires, that it should be examined with some precision.

Without inquiring into the accuracy of the distinction on which the objection is founded, it will be necessary to a just estimate of its force, first, to ascertain the real character of the government in question; secondly, to inquire how far the convention were authorized to propose such a government; and thirdly, how far the duty they owed to their country, could supply any defect of regular authority.

First. In order to ascertain the real character of the government, it may be considered in relation to the foundation on which it is to be established; to the sources from which its ordinary powers are to be drawn; to the operation of those powers; to the extent of them; and to the authority by which future changes in the government are to be introduced.

On examining the first relation, it appears, on one hand, that the constitution is to be founded on the assent and ratification of the people of America, given by deputies elected for the special purpose; but on the other, that this assent and ratification is to be given by the people, not as individuals composing one entire nation, but as composing the distinct and independent states to which they respectively belong. It is to be the assent and ratification of the several states, derived from the supreme authority in each state—the authority of the people themselves. The act, therefore, establishing the constitution, will not be a *national*, but a *federal* act.

That it will be a federal, and not a national act, as these

terms are understood by the objectors, the act of the people, as forming so many independent states, not as forming one aggregate nation, is obvious from this single consideration, that it is to result neither from the decision of a *majority* of the people of the union, nor from that of a *majority* of the states. It must result from the *unanimous* assent of the several states that are parties to it, differing no otherwise from their ordinary assent than in its being expressed, not by the legislative authority, but by that of the people themselves. Were the people regarded in this transaction as forming one nation, the will of the majority of the whole people of the United States would bind the minority; in the same manner as the majority in each state must bind the minority; and the will of the majority must be determined either by a comparison of the individual votes, or by considering the will of the majority of the states, as evidence of the will of a majority of the people of the United States. Neither of these rules has been adopted. Each state, in ratifying the constitution, is considered as a sovereign body, independent of all others, and only to be bound by its own voluntary act. In this relation, then, the new constitution will, if established, be a *federal*, and not a *national* constitution.

The next relation is, to the sources from which the ordinary powers of government are to be derived. The house of representatives will derive its powers from the people of America, and the people will be represented in the same proportion, and on the same principle, as they are in a legislature of a particular state. So far the government is *national*, not *federal*. The senate, on the other hand, will derive its powers from the states, as political and co-equal societies; and these will be represented on the principle of equality in the senate, as they now are in the existing congress. So far the government is *federal*, not *national*. The executive power will be derived from a very compound source. The immediate election of the president is to be made by the states in their political characters. The votes allotted to them are in a compound ratio, which considers them partly as distinct and co-equal societies; partly as unequal members of the same society. The eventual election, again, is to be made by that branch of the legislature which consists of the national representatives; but in this particular act, they are to be thrown into the form of individual delegations, from so many distinct and co-equal bodies politic. From this aspect of the government, it appears to be of a mixed character, presenting at least as many *federal* as *national* features.

The difference between a federal and national government, as it relates to the *operation of the government,* is, by the adversaries of the plan of the convention, supposed to consist in this, that in the former, the powers operate on the political bodies composing the confederacy, in their political capacities; in the latter, on the individual citizens composing the nation, in their individual capacities. On trying the constitution by this criterion, it falls under the *national,* not the *federal* character; though perhaps not so completely as has been understood. In several cases, and particularly in the trial of controversies to which states may be parties, they must be viewed and proceeded against in their collective and political capacities only. But the operation of the government on the people in their individual capacities, in its ordinary and most essential proceedings, will, on the whole, in the sense of its opponents, designate it, in this relation, a *national* government.

But if the government be national, with regard to the *operation* of its powers, it changes its aspect again, when we contemplate it in relation to the *extent* of its powers. The idea of a national government involves in it, not only an authority over the individual citizens, but an indefinite supremacy over all persons and things, so far as they are objects of lawful government. Among a people consolidated into one nation, this supremacy is completely vested in the national legislature. Among communities united for particular purposes, it is vested partly in the general, and partly in the municipal legislatures. In the former case, all local authorities are subordinate to the supreme; and may be controlled, directed, or abolished by it at pleasure. In the latter, the local or municipal authorities form distinct and independent portions of the supremacy, no more subject within their respective spheres, to the general authority, than the general authority is subject to them within its own sphere. In this relation, then, the proposed government cannot be deemed a *national* one; since its jurisdiction extends to certain enumerated objects only, and leaves to the several states a residuary and inviolable sovereignty over all other objects. It is true, that in controversies relating to the boundary between the two jurisdictions, the tribunal which is ultimately to decide, is to be established under the general government. But this does not change the principle of the case. The decision is to be impartially made, according to the rules of the constitution; and all the usual and most effectual precautions are taken to secure this impartiality. Some such tribunal is clearly essential to prevent an appeal to the sword, and a dissolution of the compact; and that it ought to be established under the general, rather than under the local governments; or, to speak more properly, that it could be safely established under the first alone, is a position not likely to be combated.

If we try the constitution by its last relation, to the authority by which amendments are to be made, we find it neither wholly *national*, nor wholly *federal*. Were it wholly national, the supreme and ultimate authority would reside in the *majority* of the people of the union; and this authority would be competent at all times, like that of a majority of every national society, to alter or abolish its established government. Were it wholly federal on the other hand, the concurrence of each state in the union would be essential to every alteration that would be binding on all. The mode provided by the plan of the convention, is not founded on either of these principles. In requiring more than a majority, and particularly, in computing the proportion by *states*, not by *citizens*, it departs from the *national*, and advances towards the *federal* character. In rendering the concurrence of less than the whole number of states sufficient, it loses again the *federal*, and partakes the *national* character.

The proposed constitution, therefore, even when tested by the rules laid down by its antagonists, is, in strictness, neither a national nor a federal constitution; but a composition of both. In its foundation it is federal, not national; in the sources from which the ordinary powers of the government are drawn, it is partly federal, and partly national: in the operation of these powers, it is national, not federal; in the extent of them again, it is federal, not national; and finally in the authoritative mode of introducing amendments, it is neither wholly federal, nor wholly national.

PUBLIUS.

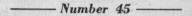

——— *Number 45* ———

James Madison

Centralization or Decentralization?

Having shown, that no one of the powers transferred to the federal government is unnecessary or improper, the next question to be considered is, whether the whole mass of them will be dangerous to the portion of authority left in the several states.

The adversaries to the plan of the convention, instead of considering in the first place, what degree of power was absolutely necessary for the purposes of the federal government, have exhausted themselves in a secondary inquiry into the possible consequences of the proposed degree of power to the governments of the particular states. But if the union, as has been shown, be essential to the security of the people of America against foreign danger; if it be essential to their security against contentions and wars among the different states; if it be essential to guard them against those violent and oppressive factions, which embitter the blessings of liberty, and against those military establishments which must gradually poison its very fountain; if, in a word, the union be essential to the happiness of the people of America, is it not preposterous, to urge as an objection to a government, without which the objects of the union cannot be attained, that such a government may derogate from the importance of the governments of the individual states? Was then the American revolution effected, was the American confederacy formed, was the precious blood of thousands spilled, and the hard-earned substance of millions lavished, not that the people of America should enjoy peace, liberty, and safety; but that the governments of the individual states, that particular municipal establishments, might enjoy a certain extent of power, and be arrayed with certain dignities and attributes of sovereignty? We have heard of the impious doctrine in the old world, that the people were made for kings, not kings for the people. Is the same doctrine to be revived in the new, in another shape, that the solid happiness of the people is to be sacrificed to the views of political institutions of a different form? It is too early for politicians to presume on our forgetting that the public good, the real welfare of the great body of the people, is the supreme object to be pursued; and that no form of government whatever has any other value, than as it may be fitted for the attainment of this object. Were the plan of the convention adverse to the public happiness, my voice would be, Reject the plan. Were the union itself inconsistent with the public happiness, it would be, Abolish the union. In like manner, as far as the sovereignty of the states cannot be reconciled to the happiness of the people, the voice of every good citizen must be, Let the former be sacrificed to the latter. How far the sacrifice is necessary, has been shown. How far the unsacrificed residue will be endangered, is the question before us.

Several important considerations have been touched in the course of these papers, which discountenance the supposition, that the operation of the federal government will by degrees prove fatal to the state governments. The more I revolve the subject, the more fully I am persuaded, that the balance is much more likely to be disturbed by the preponderancy of the last than of the first scale.

We have seen, in all the examples of ancient and modern confederacies, the strongest tendency continually betraying itself in the members, to despoil the general government of its authorities, with a very ineffectual capacity in the latter to defend itself against the encroachments. Although in most of these examples, the system has been so dissimilar from that under consideration, as greatly to weaken any inference concerning the latter, from the fate of the former; yet as the states will retain, under the proposed constitution, a very extensive portion of active sovereignty, the inference ought not to be wholly disregarded. In the Achæan league, it is probable that the federal head had a degree and species of power, which gave it a considerable likeness to the government framed by the convention. The Lycian confederacy, as far as its principles and form are transmitted, must have borne a still greater analogy to it. Yet history does not inform us, that either of them ever degenerated, or tended to degenerate, into one consolidated government. On the contrary, we know that the ruin of one of them proceeded from the incapacity of the federal authority to prevent the dissensions, and finally the disunion of the subordinate authorities. These cases are the more worthy of our attention, as the external causes by which the component parts were pressed together, were much more numerous and powerful than in our case; and consequently, less powerful ligaments within would be sufficient to bind the members to the head, and to each other.

In the feudal system, we have seen a similar propensity exemplified. Notwithstanding the want of proper sympathy in every instance between the local sovereigns and the people, and the sympathy in some instances between the general sovereign and the latter; it usually happened that the local sovereigns prevailed in the rivalship for encroachments. Had no external dangers enforced internal harmony and subordination; and particularly, had the local sovereigns possessed the affections of the people, the great kingdoms in Europe would at this time consist of as many independent princes as there were formerly feudatory barons.

The state governments will have the advantage of the federal government, whether we compare them in respect to the immediate dependence of the one on the other; to the weight of personal influence which each side will possess; to the powers respectively vested in them; to the predilection and probable support of the people; to the disposition and faculty of resisting and frustrating the measures of each other.

The state governments may be regarded as constituent and essential parts of the federal government; whilst the latter is nowise essential to the operation or organization of the former. Without the intervention of the state legislatures, the president of the United States cannot be elected at all. They must, in all cases, have a great share in his appointment, and will, perhaps, in most cases, of themselves determine it. The senate will be elected absolutely and exclusively by the state legislatures. Even the house of representatives, though drawn immediately from the people, will be chosen very much under the influence of that class of men, whose influence over the people obtains for themselves an election into the state legislatures. Thus, each of the principal branches of the federal government will owe its existence more or less to the favor of the state governments, and must consequently feel a dependence, which is much more likely to beget a disposition too obsequious, than too overbearing toward them. On the other side, the component parts of the state governments will, in no instance, be indebted for their appointment to the direct agency of the federal government, and very little, if at all, to the local influence of its members.

The number of individuals employed under the constitution of the United States, will be much smaller than the number employed under the particular states. There will consequently be less of personal influence on the side of the former than of the latter. The members of the legislative, executive, and judiciary departments of thirteen and more states; the justices of peace, officers of militia, ministerial officers of justice, with all the county, corporation, and town officers, for three millions and more of people, intermixed, and having particular acquaintance with every class and circle of people, must exceed beyond all proportion, both in number and influence, those of every description who will be employed in the administration of the federal system. Compare the members of

the three great departments, of the thirteen states, excluding
from the judiciary department the justices of peace, with the
members of the corresponding departments of the single government of the union; compare the militia officers of three millions of people, with the military and marine officers of any
establishment which is within the compass of probability, or, I
may add, of possibility; and in this view alone, we may pronounce the advantage of the states to be decisive. If the federal government is to have collectors of revenue, the state governments will have theirs also. And as those of the former will
be principally on the seacoast, and not very numerous, whilst
those of the latter will be spread over the face of the country,
and will be very numerous, the advantage in this view also
lies on the same side. It is true that the confederacy is to possess, and may exercise the power of collecting internal as well
as external taxes throughout the states: but it is probable that
this power will not be resorted to, except for supplemental
purposes of revenue; that an option will then be given to the
states to supply their quotas by previous collections of their
own; and that the eventual collection, under the immediate
authority of the union, will generally be made by the officers,
and according to the rules appointed by the several states. Indeed, it is extremely probable, that in other instances, particularly in the organization of the judicial power, the officers of
the states will be clothed with the correspondent authority of
the union. Should it happen, however, that separate collectors
of internal revenue should be appointed under the federal
government, the influence of the whole number would not
bear a comparison with that of the multitude of state officers
in the opposite scale. Within every district, to which a federal
collector would be allotted, there would not be less than thirty
or forty, or even more officers, of different descriptions, and
many of them persons of character and weight, whose influence would lie on the side of the state.

The powers delegated by the proposed constitution to the
federal government, are few and defined. Those which are to
remain in the state governments, are numerous and indefinite.
The former will be exercised principally on external objects, as

war, peace, negotiation, and foreign commerce; with which last the power of taxation will, for the most part, be connected. The powers reserved to the several states will extend to all the objects, which, in the ordinary course of affairs, concern the lives, liberties, and properties of the people; and the internal order, improvement, and prosperity of the state.

The operations of the federal government will be most extensive and important in times of war and danger; those of the state governments in times of peace and security. As the former periods will probably bear a small proportion to the latter, the state governments will here enjoy another advantage over the federal government. The more adequate indeed the federal powers may be rendered to the national defense, the less frequent will be those scenes of danger which might favor their ascendancy over the governments of the particular states.

If the new constitution be examined with accuracy and candor, it will be found that the change which it proposes, consists much less in the addition of NEW POWERS to the union, than in the invigoration of its ORIGINAL POWERS. The regulation of commerce, it is true, is a new power; but that seems to be an addition which few oppose, and from which no apprehensions are entertained. The powers relating to war and peace, armies and fleets, treaties and finance, with the other more considerable powers, are all vested in the existing congress by the articles of confederation. The proposed change does not enlarge these powers; it only substitutes a more effectual mode of administering them. The change relating to taxation, may be regarded as the most important: and yet the present congress have as complete authority to REQUIRE of the states indefinite supplies of money for the common defense and general welfare, as the future congress will have to require them of individual citizens; and the latter will be no more bound than the states themselves have been, to pay the quotas respectively taxed on them. Had the states complied punctually with the articles of confederation, or could their compliance have been enforced by as peaceable means as may be used with success toward single persons, our past experience is very far from countenancing an opinion, that the state governments would have lost their constitutional powers, and have gradually undergone an entire consolidation. To maintain that such an event would have ensued, would be to say at once, that the existence of the state governments is incompatible with any system whatever, that accomplishes the essential purposes of the union.

PUBLIUS.

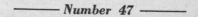 *Number 47*

James Madison

The Separation of Powers: Theory and Practice.

Having reviewed the general form of the proposed government, and the general mass of power allotted to it; I proceed to examine the particular structure of this government, and the distribution of this mass of power among its constituent parts.

One of the principal objections inculcated by the more respectable adversaries to the constitution, is its supposed violation of the political maxim, that the legislative, executive, and judiciary departments, ought to be separate and distinct. In the structure of the federal government, no regard, it is said, seems to have been paid to this essential precaution in favor of liberty. The several departments of power are distributed and blended in such a manner, as at once to destroy all symmetry and beauty of form; and to expose some of the essential parts of the edifice to the danger of being crushed by the disproportionate weight of other parts.

No political truth is certainly of greater intrinsic value, or is stamped with the authority of more enlightened patrons of liberty, than that on which the objection is founded. The accumulation of all powers, legislative, executive, and judiciary, in the same hands, whether of one, a few, or many, and whether hereditary, self-appointed, or elective, may justly be pronounced the very definition of tyranny. Were the federal constitution, therefore, really chargeable with this accumulation of power, or with a mixture of powers, having a dangerous tendency to such an accumulation, no further arguments would be necessary to inspire a universal reprobation of the system. I persuade myself, however, that it will be made apparent to every one, that the charge cannot be supported, and that the maxim on which it relies has been totally misconceived and misapplied. In order to form correct ideas on this important subject, it will be proper to investigate the sense in which the preservation of liberty requires, that the three great departments of power should be separate and distinct.

The oracle who is always consulted and cited on this subject, is the celebrated Montesquieu. If he be not the author of this invaluable precept in the science of politics, he has the merit of at least displaying and recommending it most effectually to the attention of mankind. Let us endeavor, in the first place, to ascertain his meaning on this point.

The British constitution was to Montesquieu, what Homer has been to the didactic writers on epic poetry. As the latter have considered the work of the Immortal Bard, as the perfect model from which the principles and rules of the epic art were to be drawn, and by which all similar works were to be judged: so this great political critic appears to have viewed the constitution of England as the standard, or to use his own expression, as the mirror of political liberty: and to have delivered, in the form of elementary truths, the several characteristic principles of that particular system. That we may be sure, then, not to mistake his meaning in this case, let us recur to the source from which the maxim was drawn.

On the slightest view of the British constitution, we must perceive that the legislative, executive, and judiciary departments, are by no means totally separate and distinct from each other. The executive magistrate forms an integral part of the legislative authority. He alone has the prerogative of making treaties with foreign sovereigns, which, when made, have, under certain limitations, the force of legislative acts. All the members of the judiciary department are appointed by him; can be removed by him on the address of the two houses of parliament, and form, when he pleases to consult them, one of his constitutional councils. One branch of the legislative department forms also a great constitutional council to the executive chief; as, on another hand, it is the sole depository of judicial power in cases of impeachment, and is invested with the supreme appellate jurisdiction in all other cases. The judges again are so far connected with the legislative department, as often to attend and participate in its deliberations, though not admitted to a legislative vote.

From these facts, by which Montesquieu was guided, it may clearly be inferred, that in saying, "there can be no liberty, where the legislative and executive powers are united in the same person, or body of magistrates"; or "if the power of judging, be not separated from the legislative and executive powers," he did not mean that these departments ought to have no *partial agency* in, or no *control* over, the acts of each other. His meaning, as his own words import, and still more conclusively as illustrated by the example in his eye, can amount to no more than this, that where the *whole* power of one department is exercised by the same hands which possess the *whole* power of another department, the fundamental principles of a free constitution are subverted. This would have been the case in the constitution examined by him, if the king, who is the sole executive magistrate, had possessed also the complete legislative power, or the supreme administration of justice; or if the entire legislative body had possessed the supreme judiciary, or the supreme executive authority. This, however, is not among the vices of that constitution. The magistrate, in whom the whole executive power resides, cannot of himself make a law, though he can put a negative on every law; nor administer justice in person, though he has the appointment of those who do administer it. The judges can exercise no executive prerogative, though they are shoots from the executive stock; nor any legislative function, though they may be advised with by the legislative councils. The entire legislature can perform no judiciary act; though by the joint act of two of its branches, the judges may be removed from their offices; and though one of its branches is possessed of the judicial power in the last resort. The entire legislature again can exercise no executive prerogative, though one of its branches constitutes the supreme executive magistracy; and another, on the impeachment of a third, can try and condemn all the subordinate officers in the executive department.

The reasons on which Montesquieu grounds his maxim, are a further demonstration of his meaning. "When the legislative and executive powers are united in the same person or body," says he, "there can be no liberty, because apprehensions may arise lest *the same* monarch or senate should *enact* tyrannical laws, to *execute* them in a tyrannical manner." Again, "Were the power of judging joined with the legislative, the life and liberty of the subject would be exposed to arbitrary control, for *the judge* would then be *the legislator*. Were it joined to the executive power, *the judge* might behave with all the violence of *an oppressor*." Some of these reasons are more fully explained in other passages; but briefly stated as they are here, they sufficiently establish the meaning which we have put on this celebrated maxim of this celebrated author.

If we look into the constitutions of the several states, we find, that notwithstanding the emphatical, and, in some instances, the unqualified terms in which this axiom has been laid down, there is not a single instance in which the several departments of power have been kept absolutely separate and distinct. New Hampshire, whose constitution was the last formed, seems to have been fully aware of the impossibility and inexpediency of avoiding any mixture whatever of these departments; and has qualified the doctrine by declaring, "that the legislative, executive, and judiciary powers, ought to be kept as separate from, and independent of each other, *as the nature of a free government will admit; or as is consistent with that chain of connexion, that binds the whole fabric of the constitution in one indissoluble bond of unity and amity.*" Her constitution accordingly mixes these departments in several respects. The senate, which is a branch of the legislative department, is also a judicial tribunal for the trial of impeachments. The president, who is the head of the executive department, is the presiding member also of the senate; and, besides an equal vote in all cases, has a casting vote in case of a tie. The executive head is himself eventually elective every year by the legislative department; and his council is every year chosen by and from the members of the same department. Several of the officers of state are also appointed by the legislature. And the members of the judiciary department are appointed by the executive department.

The constitution of Massachusetts has observed a sufficient, though less pointed caution, in expressing this fundamental article of liberty. It declares, "that the legislative department shall never exercise the executive and judicial powers, or either of them: the executive shall never exercise the legislative and judicial powers, or either of them; the judiciary shall never exercise the legislative and executive powers, or either of them." This declaration corresponds precisely with the doctrine of Montesquieu, as it has been explained, and is not in a single point violated by the plan of the convention. It goes no farther than to prohibit any one of the entire departments from exercising the powers of another department. In the very constitution to which it is prefixed, a partial mixture of powers has been admitted. The executive magistrate has a qualified negative on the legislative body; and the senate, which is a part of the legislature, is a court of impeachment for members both of the executive and judiciary departments. The members of the judiciary department, again, are appointable by the executive department, and removable by the same authority, on the address of the two legislative branches. Lastly, a number of the officers of government are annually appointed by the legislative department. As the appointment to offices, particularly executive offices, is in its nature an executive function, the compilers of the constitution have, in this last point at least, violated the rule established by themselves.

I pass over the constitutions of Rhode Island and Connecticut, because they were formed prior to the revolution; and even before the principle under examination had become an object of political attention.

The constitution of New York contains no declaration on this subject; but appears very clearly to have been framed with an eye to the danger of improperly blending the different departments. It gives, nevertheless, to the executive magistrate a partial control over the legislative department; and, what is more, gives a like control to the judiciary department, and even blends the executive and judiciary departments in the exercise of this control. In its council of appointment, members of the legislative are associated with the executive authority, in the appointment of officers, both executive and judiciary. And its court for the trial of impeachments and correction of errors, is to consist of one branch of the legislature and the principal members of the judiciary department.

The constitution of New Jersey has blended the different powers of government more than any of the preceding. The governor, who is the executive magistrate, is appointed by the legislature; is chancellor and ordinary, or surrogate of the state; is a member of the supreme court of appeals, and president with a casting vote of one of the legislative branches. The same legislative branch acts again as executive council of the governor, and with him constitutes the court of appeals. The members of the judiciary department are appointed by the legislative department, and removable by one branch of it on the impeachment of the other.

According to the constitution of Pennsylvania, the president, who is head of the executive department, is annually elected by a vote in which the legislative department predominates. In conjunction with an executive council, he appoints the members of the judiciary department, and forms a court of impeachment for trial of all officers, judiciary as well as executive. The judges of the supreme court, and justices of the peace seem also to be removable by the legislature; and the executive power of pardoning in certain cases to be referred to the same department. The members of the executive council are made EX OFFICIO justices of peace throughout the state.

In Delaware, the chief executive magistrate is annually elected by the legislative department. The speakers of the two legislative branches are vice presidents in the executive department. The executive chief, with six others, appointed three by each of the legislative branches, constitute the supreme court of appeals: he is joined with the legislative department in the appointment of the other judges. Throughout the states, it appears that the members of the legislature may at the same time be justices of the peace. In this state, the members of one branch of it are EX OFFICIO justices of the peace; as are also the members of the executive council. The principal officers of the executive department are appointed by the legislative; and one branch of the latter forms a court of impeachment. All officers may be removed on address of the legislature.

Maryland has adopted the maxim in the most unqualified terms; declaring that the legislative, executive, and judicial powers of government, ought to be for ever separate and distinct from each other. Her constitution, notwithstanding, makes the executive magistrate appointable by the legislative department; and the members of the judiciary by the executive department.

The language of Virginia is still more pointed on this subject. Her constitution declares, "that the legislative, executive, and judiciary departments, shall be separate and distinct; so that neither exercise the powers properly belonging to the other; nor shall any person exercise the powers of more than one of them at the same time; except that the justices of county courts shall be eligible to either house of assembly." Yet we find not only this express exception, with respect to the members of the inferior courts; but that the chief magistrate, with his executive council, are appointable by the legislature; that two members of the latter, are triennially displaced at the pleasure of the legislature; and that all the principal officers, both executive and judiciary, are filled by the same department. The executive prerogative of pardoning, also, is in one case vested in the legislative department.

The constitution of North Carolina which declares, "that the legislative, executive, and supreme judicial powers of government, ought to be for ever separate and distinct from each other," refers at the same time, to the legislative department, the appointment not only of the executive chief, but all the principal officers within both that and the judiciary department.

In South Carolina, the constitution makes the executive magistracy eligible by the legislative department. It gives to the latter, also, the appointment of the members of the judiciary department, including even justices of the peace and sheriffs; and the appointment of officers in the executive department, down to captains in the army and navy of the state.

In the constitution of Georgia, where it is declared, "that the legislative, executive, and judiciary departments shall be separate and distinct, so that neither exercise the powers properly belonging to the other," we find that the executive department is to be filled by appointments of the legislature; and the executive prerogative of pardoning to be finally exercised by the same authority. Even justices of the peace are to be appointed by the legislature.

In citing these cases in which the legislative, executive, and judiciary departments, have not been kept totally separate and distinct, I wish not to be regarded as an advocate for the particular organizations of the several state governments. I am fully aware, that among the many excellent principles which they exemplify, they carry strong marks of the haste, and still stronger of the inexperience, under which they were framed. It is but too obvious, that in some instances, the fundamental principle under consideration, has been violated by too great a mixture, and even an actual consolidation of the different powers; and that in no instance has a competent provision been made for maintaining in practice the separation delineated on paper. What I have wished to evince is, that the charge brought against the proposed constitution, of violating a sacred maxim of free government, is warranted neither by the real meaning annexed to that maxim by its author, nor by the sense in which it has hitherto been understood in America. This interesting subject will be resumed in the ensuing paper.

PUBLIUS.

──────── *Number 48* ────────

James Madison

The Separation of Powers: A Hedge Against Tyranny?

It was shown in the last paper, that the political apothegm there examined, does not require that the legislative, executive, and judiciary departments, should be wholly unconnected with each other. I shall undertake in the next place to show, that unless these departments be so far connected and blended, as to give to each a constitutional control over the others, the degree of separation which the maxim requires, as essential to a free government, can never in practice be duly maintained.

It is agreed on all sides, that the powers properly belonging to one of the departments ought not to be directly and completely administered by either of the other departments. It is equally evident, that neither of them ought to possess, directly or indirectly, an overruling influence over the others in the administration of their respective powers. It will not be denied, that power is of an encroaching nature, and that it ought to be effectually restrained from passing the limits assigned to it. After discriminating, therefore, in theory, the several classes of power, as they may in their nature be legislative, executive, or judiciary; the next, and most difficult task, is to provide some practical security for each, against the invasion of the others. What this security ought to be, is the great problem to be solved.

Will it be sufficient to mark, with precision, the boundaries of these departments, in the constitution of the government, and to trust to these parchment barriers against the encroaching spirit of power? This is the security which appears to have been principally relied on by the compilers of most of the American constitutions. But experience assures us, that the efficacy of the provision has been greatly overrated; and that some more adequate defense is indispensably necessary for the more feeble, against the more powerful members of the government. The legislative department is everywhere extending the sphere of its activity, and drawing all power into its impetuous vortex.

The founders of our republics have so much merit for the wisdom which they have displayed, that no task can be less pleasing than that of pointing out the errors into which they have fallen. A respect for truth, however, obliges us to remark, that they seem never for a moment to have turned their eyes from the danger to liberty, from the overgrown and all-grasping prerogatives of an hereditary magistrate, supported and fortified by an hereditary branch of the legislative authority. They seem never to have recollected the danger from legislative usurpations, which, by assembling all power in the same hands, must lead to the same tyranny as is threatened by executive usurpations.

In a government where numerous and extensive prerogatives are placed in the hands of an hereditary monarch, the executive department is very justly regarded as the source of danger, and watched with all the jealousy which a zeal for liberty ought to inspire. In a democracy, where a multitude of people exercise in person the legislative functions, and are continually exposed, by their incapacity for regular deliberation and concerted measures, to the ambitious intrigues of their executive magistrates, tyranny may well be apprehended on some favorable emergency, to start up in the same quarter. But in a representative republic, where the executive magistracy is carefully limited, both in the extent and the duration of its power; and where the legislative power is exercised by an assembly, which is inspired by a supposed influence over the people, with an intrepid confidence in its own strength; which is sufficiently numerous to feel all the passions which actuate a multitude; yet not so numerous as to be incapable of pursuing the objects of its passions, by means which reason prescribes; it is against the enterprising ambition of this department, that the people ought to indulge all their jealousy and exhaust all their precautions.

The legislative department derives a superiority in our governments from other circumstances. Its constitutional powers being at once more extensive, and less susceptible of precise limits, it can, with the greater facility, mask, under complicated and indirect measures, the encroachments which it makes on the co-ordinate departments. It is not infrequently a question of real nicety in legislative bodies, whether the operation of a particular measure will, or will not extend beyond the legislative sphere. On the other side, the executive power being restrained within a narrower compass, and being more simple in its nature; and the judiciary being described by landmarks, still less uncertain, projects of usurpation by either of these departments would immediately betray and defeat themselves. Nor is this all: as the legislative department alone has access to the pockets of the people, and has in some constitutions full discretion, and in all a prevailing influence over the pecuniary rewards of those who fill the other departments; a dependence is thus created in the latter, which gives still greater facility to encroachments of the former.

I have appealed to our own experience for the truth of what I advance on this subject. Were it necessary to verify this experience by particular proofs, they might be multiplied without end. I might collect vouchers in abundance from the records and archives of every state in the union. But as a more concise, and at the same time equally satisfactory evidence, I will refer to the example of two states, attested by two unexceptionable authorities.

The first example is that of Virginia, a state which, as we have seen, has expressly declared in its constitution, that the three great departments ought not to be intermixed. The authority in support of it is Mr. Jefferson, who, besides his other advantages for remarking the operation of the government,

was himself the chief magistrate of it. In order to convey fully
the ideas with which his experience had impressed him on this
subject, it will be necessary to quote a passage of some length
from his very interesting *Notes on the state of Virginia.* "All
the powers of government, legislative, executive, and judiciary, result to the legislative body. The concentrating these in
the same hands, is precisely the definition of despotic government. It will be no alleviation that these powers will be exercised by a plurality of hands, and not by a single one. One
hundred and seventy-three despots would surely be as oppressive as one. Let those who doubt it, turn their eyes on the republic of Venice. As little will it avail us, that they are chosen
by ourselves. An *elective despotism* was not the government
we fought for; but one which should not only be founded on
free principles, but in which the powers of government should
be so divided and balanced among several bodies of magistracy, as that no one could transcend their legal limits, without
being effectually checked and restrained by the others. For
this reason, that convention which passed the ordinance of
government, laid its foundation on this basis, that the legislative, executive, and judiciary departments should be separate
and distinct, so that no person should exercise the powers of
more than one of them at the same time. *But no barrier was
provided between these several powers.* The judiciary and executive members were left dependent on the legislative for
their subsistence in office, and some of them for their continuance in it. If, therefore, the legislature assumes executive and
judiciary powers, no opposition is likely to be made; nor, if
made, can be effectual; because in that case, they may put
their proceedings into the form of an act of assembly, which
will render them obligatory on the other branches. They have
accordingly, in many instances *decided rights,* which should
have been left to *judiciary controversy; and the direction of
the executive, during the whole time of their session, is becoming habitual and familiar.*"

The other state, which I shall take for an example, is Pennsylvania; and the other authority the council of censors which
assembled in the years 1783 and 1784. A part of the duty of

this body, as marked out by the constitution, was "to inquire, whether the constitution had been preserved inviolate in every part; and whether the legislative and executive branches of government had performed their duty as guardians of the people, or assumed to themselves, or exercised other or greater powers than they are entitled to by the constitution." In the execution of this trust, the council were necessarily led to a comparison of both the legislative and executive proceedings, with the constitutional powers of these departments; and from the facts enumerated, and to the truth of most of which both sides in the council subscribed, it appears, that the constitution had been flagrantly violated by the legislature in a variety of important instances.

A great number of laws had been passed, violating, without any apparent necessity, the rule requiring that all bills of a public nature shall be previously printed for the consideration of the people; although this is one of the precautions chiefly relied on by the constitution against improper acts of the legislature.

The constitutional trial by jury had been violated; and powers assumed, which had not been delegated by the constitution.

Executive powers had been usurped.

The salaries of the judges, which the constitution expressly requires to be fixed, had been occasionally varied; and cases belonging to the judiciary department frequently drawn within legislative cognizance and determination.

Those who wish to see the several particulars falling under each of these heads, may consult the journals of the council, which are in print. Some of them, it will be found, may be imputable to peculiar circumstances connected with the war: but the greater part of them may be considered as the spontaneous shoots of an ill-constituted government.

It appears also, that the executive department had not been innocent of frequent breaches of the constitution. There are three observations, however, which ought to be made on this head: *First,* A great proportion of the instances were either immediately produced by the necessities of the war, or recommended by congress, or the commander in chief: *Second,* In most of the other instances, they conformed either to the declared or the known sentiments of the legislative department: *Third,* The executive department of Pennsylvania is distinguished from that of the other states, by the number of members composing it. In this respect, it has as much affinity to a legislative assembly, as to an executive council. And being at once exempt from the restraint of an individual responsibility for the acts of the body, and deriving confidence from mutual example and joint influence; unauthorized measures would, of course, be more freely hazarded, than where the executive department is administered by a single hand, or by a few hands.

The conclusion which I am warranted in drawing from these observations is, that a mere demarcation on parchment of the constitutional limits of the several departments, is not a sufficient guard against those encroachments which lead to a tyrannical concentration of all the powers of government in the same hands.

PUBLIUS.

——— *Number 49* ———

James Madison

Doubts About Democracy.

The author of the *Notes on the state of Virginia,* quoted in the last paper, has subjoined to that valuable work, the draught of a constitution, which had been prepared in order to be laid before a convention expected to be called in 1783, by the legislature, for the establishment of a constitution for that commonwealth. The plan, like everything from the same pen, marks a turn of thinking original, comprehensive, and accurate; and is the more worthy of attention, as it equally displays a fervent attachment to republican government, and an enlightened view of the dangerous propensities against which it ought to be guarded. One of the precautions which he proposes, and on which he appears ultimately to rely as a palladium to the weaker departments of power, against the invasions of the stronger, is perhaps altogether his own, and as it immediately relates to the subject of our present inquiry, ought not to be overlooked.

His proposition is, "that whenever any two of the three branches of government shall concur in opinion, each by the voices of two-thirds of their whole number, that a convention is necessary for altering the constitution, or *correcting breaches of it*, a convention shall be called for the purpose."

As the people are the only legitimate fountain of power, and it is from them that the constitutional charter, under which the several branches of government hold their power, is derived; it seems strictly consonant to the republican theory, to recur to the same original authority, not only whenever it may be necessary to enlarge, diminish, or new-model the powers of government; but also, whenever any one of the departments may commit encroachments on the chartered authorities of the others. The several departments being perfectly co-ordinate by the terms of their common commission, neither of them, it is evident, can pretend to an exclusive or superior right of settling the boundaries between their respective powers; and how are the encroachments of the stronger to be prevented, or the wrongs of the weaker to be redressed, without an appeal to the people themselves; who, as the grantors of the commission, can alone declare its true meaning, and enforce its observance?

There is certainly great force in this reasoning, and it must be allowed to prove, that a constitutional road to the decision of the people, ought to be marked out, and kept open, for certain great and extraordinary occasions. But there appear to be insuperable objections against the proposed recurrence to the people, as a provision in all cases for keeping the several departments of power within their constitutional limits.

In the first place, the provision does not reach the case of a combination of two of the departments, against a third. If the legislative authority, which possesses so many means of operating on the motives of the other departments, should be able to gain to its interest either of the others, or even one-third of its members, the remaining department could derive no advantage from this remedial provision. I do not dwell, however, on this objection, because if may be thought to lie rather against the modification of the principle, than against the principle itself.

In the next place, it may be considered as an objection inherent in the principle, that, as every appeal to the people would carry an implication of some defect in the government, frequent appeals would, in a great measure, deprive the government of that veneration which time bestows on everything and without which perhaps the wisest and freest governments would not possess the requisite stability. If it be true that all governments rest on opinion, it is no less true, that the strength of opinion in each individual, and its practical influence on his conduct, depend much on the number which he supposes to have entertained the same opinion. The reason of man, like man himself, is timid and cautious, when left alone; and acquires firmness and confidence, in proportion to the number with which it is associated. When the examples, which fortify opinion, are ancient, as well as numerous, they are known to have a double effect. In a nation of philosophers, this consideration ought to be disregarded. A reverence for the laws, would be sufficiently inculcated by the voice of an enlightened reason. But a nation of philosophers, is as little to be expected as the philosophical race of kings wished for by Plato. And in every other nation, the most rational government will not find it a superfluous advantage to have the prejudices of the community on its side.

The danger of disturbing the public tranquillity, by interesting too strongly the public passions, is a still more serious objection against a frequent reference of constitutional questions, to the decision of the whole society. Notwithstanding the success which has attended the revisions of our established forms of government, and which does so much honor to the virtue and intelligence of the people of America, it must be confessed, that the experiments are of too ticklish a nature to be unnecessarily multiplied. We are to recollect, that all the existing constitutions were formed in the midst of a danger which repressed the passions most unfriendly to order and concord; of an enthusiastic confidence of the people in their patriotic leaders, which stifled the ordinary diversity of opinions on great national questions; of an universal ardor for new and opposite forms, produced by an universal resentment and indignation against the ancient government; and whilst no spirit of party, connected with the changes to be made, or the abuses to be reformed, could mingle its leaven in the operation. The future situations in which we must expect to be usually placed, do not present any equivalent security against the danger which is apprehended.

But the greatest objection of all is, that the decisions which would probably result from such appeals, would not answer the purpose of maintaining the constitutional equilibrium of the government. We have seen that the tendency of republican governments is, to an aggrandizement of the legislative, at the expense of the other departments. The appeals to the people, therefore, would usually be made by the executive and judiciary departments. But whether made by one side or the other, would each side enjoy equal advantages on the trial? Let us view their different situations. The members of the executive and judiciary departments, are few in number, and can be personally known to a small part only of the people. The latter, by the mode of their appointment, as well as by the nature and permanency of it, are too far removed from the people to share much in their prepossessions. The former are generally the objects of jealousy; and their administration is always liable to be discolored and rendered unpopular. The members of the legislative department, on the other hand, are numerous. They are distributed and dwell among the people at large. Their connections of blood, of friendship, and of acquaintance, embrace a great proportion of the most influential part of the society. The nature of their public trust implies a personal weight with the people, and that they are more immediately the confidential guardians of their rights and liberties. With these advantages, it can hardly be supposed, that the adverse party would have an equal chance for a favorable issue.

But the legislative party would not only be able to plead their cause most successfully with the people: They would probably be constituted themselves the judges. The same influence which had gained them an election into the legislature, would gain them a seat in the convention. If this should not be the case with all, it would probably be the case with many, and pretty certainly with those leading characters, on whom everything depends in such bodies. The convention, in short, would be composed chiefly of men who had been, who actually were, or who expected to be, members of the department whose conduct was arraigned. They would consequently be parties to the very question to be decided by them.

It might, however, sometimes happen, that appeals would be made under circumstances less adverse to the executive and judiciary departments. The usurpations of the legislature might be so flagrant and so sudden, as to admit of no specious coloring. A strong party among themselves might take side with the other branches. The executive power might be in the hands of a peculiar favorite of the people. In such a posture of things, the public decision might be less swayed by prepossessions in favor of the legislative party. But still it could never be expected to turn on the true merits of the question. It would inevitably be connected with the spirit, of parties pre-existing, or springing out of the question itself. It would be connected with persons of distinguished character, and extensive influence in the community. It would be pronounced by the very men who had been agents in, or opponents of the measures, to which the decision would relate. The *passions,* therefore, not the *reason,* of the public, would sit in judgment. But it is the reason of the public alone, that ought to control and regulate the government. The passions ought to be controlled and regulated by the government.

We found in the last paper, that mere declarations in the written constitution, are not sufficient to restrain the several departments within their legal limits. It appears in this, that occasional appeals to the people, would be neither a proper, nor an effectual provision, for that purpose. How far the provisions of a different nature contained in the plan above quoted, might be adequate, I do not examine. Some of them are unquestionably founded on sound political principles, and all of them are framed with singular ingenuity and precision.

PUBLIUS.

————— *Number 51* —————

James Madison

The Social Foundations of Political Freedom.

To what expedient then shall we finally resort, for maintaining in practice the necessary partition of power among the several departments, as laid down in the constitution? The only answer that can be given is, that as all these exterior provisions are found to be inadequate, the defect must be supplied, by so contriving the interior structure of the government, as that its several constituent parts may, by their mutual relations, be the means of keeping each other in their proper places. Without presuming to undertake a full development of this important idea, I will hazard a few general observations, which may, perhaps, place it in a clearer light, and enable us to form a more correct judgment of the principles and structure of the government planned by the convention.

In order to lay a due foundation for that separate and distinct exercise of the different powers of government, which, to a certain extent, is admitted on all hands to be essential to the preservation of liberty, it is evident that each department should have a will of its own; and consequently should be so constituted, that the members of each should have as little agency as possible in the appointment of the members of the others. Were this principle rigorously adhered to, it would require that all the appointments for the supreme executive, legislative, and judiciary magistracies, should be drawn from the same fountain of authority, the people, through channels, having no communication whatever with one another. Perhaps such a plan of constructing the several departments, would be less difficult in practice, than it may in contemplation appear. Some difficulties, however, and some additional expense, would attend the execution of it. Some deviations, therefore, from the principle must be admitted. In the constitution of the judiciary department in particular, it might be inexpedient to insist rigorously on the principle, first, because peculiar qualifications being essential in the members, the primary consideration ought to be to select that mode of choice, which best secures these qualifications; secondly, because the permanent tenure by which the appointments are held in that department, must soon destroy all sense of dependence on the authority conferring them.

It is equally evident, that the members of each department should be as little dependent as possible on those of the others, for the emoluments annexed to their offices. Were the executive magistrate, or the judges, not independent of the legislature in this particular, their independence in every other, would be merely nominal.

But the great security against a gradual concentration of the several powers in the same department, consists in giving to those who administer each department, the necessary constitutional means, and personal motives, to resist encroachments of the others. The provision for defense must in this, as in all other cases, be made commensurate to the danger of attack. Ambition must be made to counteract ambition. The interest of the man must be connected with the constitutional rights of the place. It may be a reflection on human nature, that such devices should be necessary to control the abuses of government. But what is government itself, but the greatest of all reflections on human nature? If men were angels, no government would be necessary. If angels were to govern men, neither external nor internal controls on government would be necessary. In framing a government, which is to be administered by men over men, the great difficulty lies in this: You must first enable the government to control the governed; and in the next place, oblige it to control itself. A dependence on the people is, no doubt, the primary control on the government; but experience has taught mankind the necessity of auxiliary precautions.

This policy of supplying by opposite and rival interests, the defect of better motives, might be traced through the whole system of human affairs, private as well as public. We see it particularly displayed in all the subordinate distributions of power; where the constant aim is, to divide and arrange the several offices in such a manner, as that each may be a check on the other; that the private interest of every individual, may be a sentinel over the public rights. These inventions of prudence cannot be less requisite to the distribution of the supreme powers of the state.

But it is not possible to give to each department an equal power of self-defense. In republican government, the legislative authority necessarily predominates. The remedy for this inconveniency is, to divide the legislature into different branches; and to render them by different modes of election, and different principles of action, as little connected with each other, as the nature of their common functions, and their common dependence on the society will admit. It may even be necessary to guard against dangerous encroachments, by still further precautions. As the weight of the legislative authority requires that it should be thus divided, the weakness of the executive may require, on the other hand, that it should be fortified. An absolute negative on the legislature, appears, at first view, to be the natural defense with which the executive magistrate should be armed. But perhaps it would be neither altogether safe, nor alone sufficient. On ordinary occasions, it might not be exerted with the requisite firmness; and on extraordinary occasions, it might be perfidiously abused. May not this defect of an absolute negative be supplied by some qualified connection between this weaker department, and the weaker branch of the stronger department, by which the latter may be led to support the constitutional rights of the former, without being too much detached from the rights of its own department?

If the principles on which these observations are founded be just, as I persuade myself they are, and they be applied as a criterion to the several state constitutions, and to the federal constitution, it will be found, that if the latter does not perfectly correspond with them, the former are infinitely less able to bear such a test.

There are, moreover, two considerations particularly applicable to the federal system of America, which place it in a very interesting point of view.

First. In a single republic, all the power surrendered by the people is submitted to the administration of a single government; and the usurpations are guarded against, by a division of the government into distinct and separate departments. In the compound republic of America, the power surrendered by the people is first divided between two distinct governments, and then the portion allotted to each subdivided among distinct and separate departments. Hence a double security arises to the rights of the people. The different governments will control each other; at the same time that each will be controlled by itself.

Second. It is of great importance in a republic, not only to guard the society against the oppression of its rulers; but to guard one part of the society against the injustice of the other part. Different interests necessarily exist in different classes of citizens. If a majority be united by a common interest, the rights of the minority will be insecure. There are but two methods of providing against this evil: The one by creating a will in the community independent of the majority, that is, of the society itself; the other by comprehending in the society so many separate descriptions of citizens, as will render an unjust combination of a majority of the whole very improbable, if not impracticable. The first method prevails in all governments possessing an hereditary or self-appointed authority. This, at best, is but a precarious security; because a power independent of the society may as well espouse the unjust views of the major, as the rightful interests of the minor party, and may possibly be turned against both parties. The second method will be exemplified in the federal republic of the United States. Whilst all authority in it will be derived from, and dependent on the society, the society itself will be broken into so many parts, interests, and classes of citizens, that the rights of individuals, or of the minority, will be in little danger from interested combinations of the majority. In a free government, the security for civil rights must be the same as that for religious rights. It consists in the one case in the multiplicity of interests, and in the other, in the multiplicity of sects. The degree of security in both cases will depend on the number of interests and sects; and this may be presumed to depend on the extent of country and number of people comprehended under the same government. This view of the subject must particularly recommend a proper federal system, to all the sincere and considerate friends of republican government: since it shows that, in exact proportion, as the territory of the union may be formed into more circumscribed confederacies, or states, oppressive combinations of a majority will be facilitated, the best security under the republican form, for the rights of every class of citizens, will be diminished; and consequently, the stability and independence of some member of the government, the only other security must be proportionably increased. Justice is the end of government. It is the end of civil society. It ever has been, and ever will be pursued, until it be obtained, or until liberty be lost in the pursuit. In a society, under the forms of which the stronger faction can readily unite and oppress the weaker, anarchy may as truly be said to reign, as in a state of nature where the weaker individual is not secured against the violence of the stronger: And as in the latter state even the stronger individuals are prompted by the uncertainty of their condition, to submit to a government, which may protect the weak as well as themselves: so in the former state, will the more powerful factions be gradually induced by a like motive to wish for a government which will protect all parties, the weaker as well as the more powerful. It can be little doubted, that if the state of Rhode Island was separated from the confederacy, and left to itself, the insecurity of rights under the popular form of government within such narrow limits, would be displayed by such reiterated oppressions of factious majorities, that some power altogether independent of the people, would soon be called for by the voice of the very factions whose misrule had proved the necessity of it. In the extended republic of the United States, and among the great variety of interests, parties, and sects, which it embraces, a coalition of a majority of the whole society could seldom take place upon any other principles, than those of justice and the general good: Whilst there being thus less danger to a minor from the will of the major party, there must be less pretext also, to provide for the security of the former, by introducing into the government a will not dependent on the latter: or, in other words, a will independent of the society itself. It is no less certain than it is important, notwithstanding the contrary opinions which have been entertained, that the larger the society, provided it lie within a practicable sphere, the more duly capable it will be of self-government. And happily for the republican cause, the practicable sphere may be carried to a very great extent by a judicious modification and mixture of the federal principle.

PUBLIUS.

 *Number 62*

James Madison

The Senate.

The heads under which this member [the Senate] of the government may be considered are—I. The qualification of senators; II. The appointment of them by the state legislatures;

III. The equality of representation in the senate; IV. The number of senators, and the term for which they are to be elected; V. The powers vested in the senate.

I. The qualifications proposed for senators, as distinguished from those of representatives, consist in a more advanced age and a longer period of citizenship. A senator must be thirty years of age at least; as a representative must be twenty-five. And the former must have been a citizen nine years; as seven years are required for the latter. The propriety of these distinctions is explained by the nature of the senatorial trust; which, requiring greater extent of information and stability of character, requires at the same time, that the senator should have reached a period of life most likely to supply these advantages; and which, participating immediately in transactions with foreign nations, ought to be exercised by none, who are not thoroughly weaned from the prepossessions and habits, incident to foreign birth and education. The term of nine years appears to be a prudent mediocrity between a total exclusion of adopted citizens, whose merit and talents may claim a share in the public confidence; and an indiscriminate and hasty admission of them, which might create a channel for foreign influence on the national councils.

II. It is equally unnecessary to dilate on the appointment of senators by the state legislators. Among the various modes which might have been devised for constituting this branch of the government, that which has been proposed by the convention is probably the most congenial with the public opinion. It is recommended by the double advantage of favoring a select appointment, and of giving to the state governments such an agency in the formation of the federal government, as must secure the authority of the former, and may form a convenient link between the two systems.

III. The equality of representation in the senate is another point, which, being evidently the result of compromise between the opposite pretensions of the large and the small states, does not call for much discussion. If indeed it be right, that among a people thoroughly incorporated into one nation, every district ought to have a *proportional* share in the government: and that among independent and sovereign states bound together by a simple league, the parties, however unequal in size, ought to have an *equal* share in the common councils, it does not appear to be without some reason, that in a compound republic, partaking both of the national and federal character, the government ought to be founded on a mixture of the principles of proportional and equal representation. But it is superfluous to try, by the standard of theory, a part of the constitution which is allowed on all hands to be the result, not of theory, but "of a spirit of amity, and that mutual deference and concession which the peculiarity of our political situation rendered indispensable." A common government, with powers equal to its objects, is called for by the voice, and still more loudly by the political situation, of America. A government founded on principles more consonant to the wishes of the larger states, is not likely to be obtained from the smaller states. The only option then for the former lies between the proposed government, and a government still more objectionable. Under this alternative the advice of prudence must be, to embrace the lesser evil; and, instead of indulging as fruitless anticipation of the possible mischiefs which may ensue, to contemplate rather the advantageous consequences which may qualify the sacrifice.

In this spirit it may be remarked, that the equal vote allowed to each state, is at once a constitutional recognition of the portion of sovereignty remaining in the individual states, and an instrument for preserving that residuary sovereignty. So far the equality ought to be no less acceptable to the large than to the small states; since they are not less solicitous to guard by every possible expedient against an improper consolidation of the states into one simple republic.

Another advantage accruing from this ingredient in the constitution of the senate is, the additional impediment it must prove against improper acts of legislation. No law or resolution can now be passed without the concurrence, first, of a majority of the people, and then, of a majority of the states. It must be acknowledged that this complicated check on legislation may, in some instances, be injurious as well as beneficial; and that the peculiar defense which it involves in favor of the smaller states, would be more rational, if any interests common to them, and distinct from those of the other states, would otherwise be exposed to peculiar danger. But as the larger states will always be able, by their power over the supplies, to defeat unreasonable exertions of this prerogative of the lesser states; and as the facility and excess of law-making seem to be the diseases to which our governments are most liable, it is not impossible, that this part of the constitution may be more convenient in practice than it appears to many in contemplation.

IV. The number of senators, and the duration of their appointment, come next to be considered. In order to form an accurate judgment on both these points, it will be proper to inquire into the purposes which are to be answered by the senate; and, in order to ascertain these, it will be necessary to review the inconveniences which a republic must suffer from the want of such an institution.

First. It is a misfortune incident to republican government, though in a less degree than to other governments, that those who administer it may forget their obligations to their constituents, and prove unfaithful to their important trust. In this point of view, a senate, as a second branch of the legislative assembly, distinct from, and dividing the power with, a first, must be in all cases a salutary check on the government. It doubles the security to the people by requiring the concurrence of two distinct bodies in schemes of usurpation or perfidy, where the ambition or corruption of one would otherwise be sufficient. This is a precaution founded on such clear principles, and now so well understood in the United States, that it would be more than superfluous to enlarge on it. I will barely remark, that, as the improbability of sinister combinations will be in proportion to the dissimilarity in the genius of the two bodies, it must be politic to distinguish them from each other by every circumstance which will consist with a due harmony in all proper measures, and with the genuine principles of republican government.

Second. The necessity of a senate is not less indicated by the propensity of all single and numerous assemblies, to yield to the impulse of sudden and violent passions, and to be seduced by factious leaders into intemperate and pernicious resolutions. Examples on this subject might be cited without number; and from proceedings within the United States, as well as from the history of other nations. But a position that will not be contradicted need not be proved. All that need be remarked is, that a body which is to correct this infirmity ought itself to be free from it, and consequently ought to be less numerous. It ought, moreover, to possess great firmness, and consequently ought to hold its authority by a tenure of considerable duration.

Third. Another defect to be supplied by a senate lies in a want of due acquaintance with the objects and principles of legislation. It is not possible that an assembly of men, called, for the most part, from pursuits of a private nature, continued in appointments for a short time, and led by no permanent motive to devote the intervals of public occupation to a study of the laws, the affairs, and the comprehensive interests of their country, should, if left wholly to themselves, escape a variety of important errors in the exercise of their legislative trust. It may be affirmed, on the best grounds, that no small share of the present embarrassments of America is to be charged on the blunders of our governments; and that these have proceeded from the heads rather than the hearts of most of the authors of them. What indeed are all the repealing, explaining, and amending laws which fill and disgrace our voluminous codes, but so many monuments of deficient wisdom; so many impeachments exhibited by each succeeding, against each preceding, session; so many admonitions to the people, of the value of those aids, which may be expected from a well constituted senate?

A good government implies two things; first, fidelity to the object of government, which is the happiness of the people; secondly, a knowledge of the means by which that object can be best attained. Some governments are deficient in both these qualities: Most governments are deficient in the first. I scruple not to assert, that, in the American governments, too little attention has been paid to the last. The federal constitution avoids this error: and what merits particular notice, it provides for the last in a mode which increases the security for the first.

Fourth. The mutability in the public councils, arising from a rapid succession of new members, however qualified they may be, points out, in the strongest manner, the necessity of some stable institution in the government. Every new election in the states is found to change one-half of the representatives. From this change of men must proceed a change of opinions; and from a change of opinions, a change of measures. But a continual change even of good measures is inconsistent with every rule of prudence, and every prospect of success. The remark is verified in private life, and becomes more just as well as more important, in national transactions.

To trace the mischievous effects of a mutable government would fill a volume. I will hint a few only, each of which will be perceived to be a source of innumerable others.

In the first place, it forfeits the respect and confidence of other nations, and all the advantages connected with national character. An individual who is observed to be inconstant to his plans, or perhaps to carry on his affairs without any plan at all, is marked at once by all prudent people, as a speedy victim to his own unsteadiness and folly. His more friendly neighbors may pity him, but all will decline to connect their fortunes with his; and not a few will seize the opportunity of making their fortunes out of his. One nation is to another what one individual is to another; with this melancholy distinction perhaps, that the former, with fewer of the benevolent emotions than the latter, are under fewer restraints also from taking undue advantage of the indiscretions of each other. Every nation, consequently, whose affairs betray a want of wisdom and stability, may calculate on every loss which can be sustained from the more systematic policy of its wiser neighbors. But the best instruction on this subject is unhappily conveyed to America by the example of her own situation. She finds that she is held in no respect by her friends; that she is the derision of her enemies; and that she is a prey to every nation which has an interest in speculating on her fluctuating councils and embarrassed affairs.

The internal effects of a mutable policy are still more calamitous. It poisons the blessings of liberty itself. It will be of little avail to the people that the laws are made by men of their own choice, if the laws be so voluminous that they cannot be read, or so incoherent that they cannot be understood: if they be repealed or revised before they are promulgated, or undergo such incessant changes, that no man who knows what the law is today, can guess what it will be tomorrow. Law is defined to be a rule of action; but how can that be a rule which is little known and less fixed?

Another effect of public instability is the unreasonable advantage it gives to the sagacious, the enterprising, and the monied few, over the industrious and uninformed mass of the people. Every new regulation concerning commerce or revenue, or in any manner affecting the value of the different species of property, presents a new harvest to those who watch the change, and can trace its consequences; a harvest, reared not by themselves, but by the toils and cares of the great body of their fellow-citizens. This is the state of things in which it may be said, with some truth, that laws are made for the *few*, not for the *many*.

In another point of view, great injury results from an unstable government. The want of confidence in the public councils, damps every useful undertaking; the success and profit of which may depend on a continuance of existing arrangements. What prudent merchant will hazard his fortunes in any new branch of commerce when he knows not but that his plans may be rendered unlawful before they can be executed? What farmer or manufacturer will lay himself out for the encouragement given to any particular cultivation or establishment, when he can have no assurance that his preparatory labors and advances will not render him a victim to an inconstant government? In a word, no great improvement or laudable enterprise can go forward which requires the auspices of a steady system of national policy.

But the most deplorable effect of all is that diminution of

attachment and reverence, which steals into the hearts of the people toward a political system which betrays so many marks of infirmity, and disappoints so many of their flattering hopes. No government, any more than an individual, will long be respected, without being truly respectable; nor be truly respectable without possessing a certain portion of order and stability.

PUBLIUS.

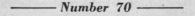

———— *Number 70* ————

Alexander Hamilton

The President.

There is an idea, which is not without its advocates, that a vigorous executive is inconsistent with the genius of republican government. The enlightened well-wishers to this species of government must at least hope that the supposition is destitute of foundation; since they can never admit its truth, without, at the same time, admitting the condemnation of their own principles. Energy in the executive is a leading character in the definition of good government. It is essential to the protection of the community against foreign attacks: It is not less essential to the steady administration of the laws, to the protection of property against those irregular and high-handed combinations, which sometimes interrupt the ordinary course of justice, to the security of liberty against the enterprises and assaults of ambition, of faction, and of anarchy. Every man, the least conversant in Roman story, knows how often that republic was obliged to take refuge in the absolute power of a single man, under the formidable title of dictator, as well against the intrigues of ambitious individuals, who aspired to the tyranny, and the seditions of whole classes of the community, whose conduct threatened the existence of all government, as against the invasions of external enemies, who menaced the conquest and destruction of Rome.

There can be no need, however, to multiply arguments or examples on this head. A feeble executive implies a feeble execution of the government. A feeble execution is but another phrase for a bad execution: and a government ill executed, whatever it may be in theory, must be, in practice, a bad government.

Taking it for granted, therefore, that all men of sense will agree in the necessity of an energetic executive, it will only remain to inquire, what are the ingredients which constitute this energy? How far can they be combined with those other ingredients, which constitute safety in the republican sense? And how far does this combination characterize the plan which has been reported by the convention?

The ingredients which constitute energy in the executive are, unity; duration; an adequate provision for its support; competent powers.

The ingredients which constitute safety in the republican sense are, a due dependence on the people; a due responsibility.

Those politicians and statesmen, who have been the most celebrated for the soundness of their principles, and for the justness of their views, have declared in favor of a single executive, and a numerous legislature. They have, with great propriety, considered energy as the most necessary qualification of the former, and have regarded this as most applicable to power in a single hand; while they have, with equal propriety, considered the latter as best adapted to deliberation and wisdom, and best calculated to conciliate the confidence of the people, and to secure their privileges and interests.

That unity is conducive to energy will not be disputed. Decision, activity, secrecy, and dispatch, will generally characterize the proceedings of one man, in a much more eminent degree than the proceedings of any greater number; and in proportion as the number is increased, these qualities will be diminished.

This unity may be destroyed in two ways; either by vesting

the power in two or more magistrates, of equal dignity and authority; or by vesting it ostensibly in one man, subject, in whole or in part, to the control and co-operation of others, in the capacity of counsellors to him. Of the first, the two consuls of Rome may serve as an example; of the last, we shall find examples in the constitutions of several of the states. New York and New Jersey, if I recollect right, are the only states which have intrusted the executive authority wholly to single men. Both these methods of destroying the unity of the executive have their partisans; but the votaries of an executive council are the most numerous. They are both liable, if not to equal, to similar objections, and may in most lights be examined in conjunction.

The experience of other nations will afford little instruction on this head. As far, however, as it teaches anything, it teaches us not to be enamored of plurality in the executive. We have seen that the Achæans, on an experiment of two prætors, were induced to abolish one. The Roman history records many instances of mischiefs to the republic from the dissensions between the consuls, and between the military tribunes, who were at times substituted to the consuls. But it gives us no specimens of any peculiar advantages derived to the state, from the plurality of those magistrates. That the dissensions between them were not more frequent or more fatal, is matter of astonishment; until we advert to the singular position in which the republic was almost continually placed, and to the prudent policy pointed out by the circumstances of the state, and pursued by the consuls, of making a division of the government between them. The patricians, engaged in a perpetual struggle with the plebeians, for the preservation of their ancient authorities and dignities; the consuls, who were generally chosen out of the former body, were commonly united by the personal interest they had in the defense of the privileges of their order. In addition to this motive of union, after the arms of the republic had considerably expanded the bounds of its empire, it became an established custom with the consuls to divide the administration between themselves by lot; one of them remaining at Rome to govern the city and its environs; the other taking the command in the more distant provinces. This expedient must, no doubt, have had great influence in preventing those collisions and rivalships which might otherwise have embroiled the republic.

But quitting the dim light of historical research, and attaching ourselves purely to the dictates of reason and good sense, we shall discover much greater cause to reject, than to approve, the idea of plurality in the executive, under any modification whatever.

Wherever two or more persons are engaged in any common enterprise or pursuit, there is always danger of difference of opinion. If it be a public trust or office, in which they are clothed with equal dignity and authority, there is peculiar danger of personal emulation and even animosity. From either, and especially from all these causes, the most bitter dissensions are apt to spring. Whenever these happen, they lessen the respectability, weaken the authority, and distract the plans and operations of those whom they divide. If they should unfortunately assail the supreme executive magistracy of a country, consisting of a plurality of persons, they might impede or frustrate the most important measures of the government, in the most critical emergencies of the state. And what is still worse, they might split the community into violent and irreconcilable factions, adhering differently to the different individuals who composed the magistracy.

Men often oppose a thing merely because they have had no agency in planning it, or because it may have been planned by those whom they dislike. But if they have been consulted, and have happened to disapprove, opposition then becomes, in their estimation, an indispensable duty of self-love. They seem to think themselves bound in honor, and by all the motives of personal infallibility, to defeat the success of what has been resolved upon, contrary to their sentiments. Men of upright and benevolent tempers have too many opportunities of remarking with horror, to what desperate lengths this disposition is sometimes carried, and how often the great interests of society are sacrificed to the vanity, to the conceit, and to the obstinacy of individuals, who have credit enough to make their passions and their caprices interesting to mankind. Perhaps the question now before the public may, in its consequences, afford melancholy proofs of the effects of this despicable frailty, or rather detestable vice in the human character.

Upon the principles of a free government, inconveniences from the source just mentioned, must necessarily be submitted to in the formation of the legislature; but it is unnecessary, and therefore unwise, to introduce them into the constitution of the executive. It is here, too, that they may be most pernicious. In the legislature, promptitude of decision is oftener an evil than a benefit. The differences of opinion, and the jarrings of parties in that department of the government, though they may sometimes obstruct salutary plans, yet often promote deliberation and circumspection; and serve to check excesses in the majority. When a resolution, too, is once taken, the opposition must be at an end. That resolution is a law, and resistance to it punishable. But no favorable circumstances palliate, or atone for the disadvantages of dissension in the executive department. Here they are pure and unmixed. There is no point at which they cease to operate. They serve to embarrass and weaken the execution of the plan or measure to which they relate, from the first step to the final conclusion of it. They constantly counteract those qualities in the executive, which are the most necessary ingredients in its composition—vigor and expedition; and this without any counterbalancing good. In the conduct of war, in which the energy of the executive is the bulwark of the national security, everything would be to be apprehended from its plurality.

It must be confessed, that these observations apply with principal weight to the first case supposed, that is, to a plurality of magistrates of equal dignity and authority; a scheme, the advocates for which are not likely to form a numerous sect: But they apply, though not with equal, yet with considerable weight, to the project of a council, whose concurrence is made constitutionally necessary to the operations of the ostensible executive. An artful cabal in that council would be able to distract and to enervate the whole system of administration. If no such cabal should exist, the mere diversity of views and opinions would alone be sufficient to tincture the exercise of the executive authority with a spirit of habitual feebleness and dilatoriness.

But one of the weightiest objections to a plurality in the executive, and which lies as much against the last as the first plan, is, that it tends to conceal faults, and destroy responsibility. Responsibility is of two kinds, to censure and to punishment. The first is the most important of the two; especially in an elective office. Men in public trust will much oftener act in such a manner as to render them unworthy of being any longer trusted, than in such a manner as to make them obnoxious to legal punishment. But the multiplication of the executive adds to the difficulty of detection in either case. It often becomes impossible, amid mutual accusations, to determine on whom the blame or the punishment of a pernicious measure, or series of pernicious measures, ought really to fall. It is shifted from one to another with so much dexterity, and under such plausible appearances, that the public opinion is left in suspense about the real author. The circumstances which may have led to any national miscarriage or misfortune, are sometimes so complicated, that where there are a number of actors who may have had different degrees and kinds of agency, though we may clearly see upon the whole that there has been mismanagement, yet it may be impracticable to pronounce, to whose account the evil which may have been incurred is truly chargeable.

"I was overruled by my council. The council were so divided in their opinions that it was impossible to obtain any better resolution on the point." These and similar pretexts are constantly at hand, whether true or false. And who is there that will either take the trouble, or incur the odium, of a strict scrutiny into the secret springs of the transaction? Should there be found a citizen zealous enough to undertake the unpromising task, if there happen to be a collusion between the parties concerned, how easy is it to clothe the circumstances with so much ambiguity, as to render it uncertain what was the precise conduct of any of those parties?

In the single instance in which the governor of this state is coupled with a council, that is, in the appointment to offices, we have seen the mischiefs of it in the view now under consideration. Scandalous appointments to important offices have been made. Some cases indeed have been so flagrant, that ALL PARTIES have agreed in the impropriety of the thing. When inquiry has been made, the blame has been laid by the governor on the members of the council; who on their part have charged it upon his nomination: while the people remain altogether at a loss to determine by whose influence their interests have been committed to hands so manifestly improper. In tenderness to individuals, I forbear to descend to particulars.

It is evident from these considerations, that the plurality of the executive tends to deprive the people of the two greatest securities they can have for the faithful exercise of any delegated power. *First*. The restraints of public opinion, which lose their efficacy as well on account of the division of the censure attendant on bad measures among a number, as on account of the uncertainty on whom it ought to fall; and *secondly*, the opportunity of discovering with facility and clearness the misconduct of the persons they trust, in order either to their removal from office, or to their actual punishment, in cases which admit of it.

In England, the king is a perpetual magistrate; and it is a maxim which has obtained for the sake of the public peace, that he is unaccountable for his administration, and his person sacred. Nothing, therefore, can be wiser in that kingdom, than to annex to the king a constitutional council, who may be responsible to the nation for the advice they give. Without this there would be no responsibility whatever in the executive department, an idea inadmissible in a free government. But even there the king is not bound by the resolutions of his council, though they are answerable for the advice they give. He is the absolute master of his own conduct in the exercise of his office; and may observe or disregard the counsel given to him at his sole discretion.

But in a republic, where every magistrate ought to be personally responsible for his behavior in office, the reason which in the British constitution dictates the propriety of a council, not only ceases to apply, but turns against the institution. In the monarchy of Great Britain, it furnishes a substitute for the prohibited responsibility of the chief magistrate; which serves in some degree as a hostage to the national justice for his good behavior. In the American republic it would serve to destroy, or would greatly diminish the intended and necessary responsibility of the chief magistrate himself.

The idea of a council to the executive, which has so generally obtained in the state constitutions, has been derived from that maxim of republican jealousy which considers power as safer in the hands of a number of men than of a single man. If the maxim should be admitted to be applicable to the case, I should contend that the advantage on that side would not counterbalance the numerous disadvantages on the opposite side. But I do not think the rule at all applicable to the executive power. I clearly concur in opinion in this particular with a writer whom the celebrated Junius pronounces to be "deep, solid, and ingenius," that "the executive power is more easily confined when it is ONE:" That it is far more safe there should be a single object for the jealousy and watchfulness of the people; in a word, that all multiplication of the executive, is rather dangerous than friendly to liberty.

A little consideration will satisfy us, that the species of security sought for in the multiplication of the executive, is unattainable. Numbers must be so great as to render combination difficult; or they are rather a source of danger than of security. The united credit and influence of several individuals must be more formidable to liberty than the credit and influence of either of them separately. When power, therefore, is placed in the hands of so small a number of men, as to admit of their interests and views being easily combined in a common enterprise, by an artful leader, it becomes more liable to abuse, and more dangerous when abused, than if it be lodged in the hands of one man; who, from the very circumstance of his being alone, will be more narrowly watched and more readily suspected, and who cannot unite so great a mass of influence as when he is associated with others. The decemvirs of Rome, whose name denotes their number, were more to be dreaded in their usurpation than any ONE of them would have been. No person would think of proposing an executive much more numerous than that body; from six, to a dozen, have been suggested for the number of the council. The extreme of these numbers is not too great for an easy combination; and from such a combination America would have more to fear, than from the ambition of any single individual. A council to a magistrate, who is himself responsible for what he does, are generally nothing better than a clog upon his good intentions; are often the instruments and accomplices of his bad, and are almost always a cloak to his faults.

I forbear to dwell upon the subject of expense; though it be evident that if the council should be numerous enough to answer the principal end, aimed at by the institution, the salaries of the members, who must be drawn from their homes to reside at the seat of government, would form an item in the catalogue of public expenditures, too serious to be incurred for an object of equivocal utility.

I will only add, that prior to the appearance of the constitution, I rarely met with an intelligent man from any of the states, who did not admit as the result of experience, that the unity of the executive of this state was one of the best of the distinguishing features of our constitution.

PUBLIUS.

——— *Number 78* ———

Alexander Hamilton

The Supreme Court.

We proceed now to an examination of the judiciary department of the proposed government.

In unfolding the defects of the existing confederation, the utility and necessity of a federal judicature have been clearly pointed out. It is the less necessary to recapitulate the considerations there urged; as the propriety of the institution in the abstract is not disputed: The only questions which have been raised being relative to the manner of constituting it, and to its extent. To these points, therefore, our observations shall be confined.

The manner of constituting it seems to embrace these several objects: 1st. The mode of appointing the judges: 2nd. The tenure by which they are to hold their places: 3rd. The partition of the judiciary authority between different courts, and their relations to each other.

First. As to the mode of appointing the judges: This is the same with that of appointing the officers of the union in general, and has been so fully discussed . . . that nothing can be said here which would not be useless repetition.

Second. As to the tenure by which the judges are to hold their places: This chiefly concerns their duration in office; the provisions for their support; the precautions for their responsibility.

According to the plan of the convention, all the judges who may be appointed by the United States are to hold their offices *during good behavior;* which is conformable to the most approved of the state constitutions—among the rest, to that of this state. Its propriety having been drawn into question by the adversaries of that plan, is no light symptom of the rage for objection, which disorders their imaginations and judgments. The standard of good behavior for the continuance in office of the judicial magistracy is certainly one of the most valuable of the modern improvements in the practice of government. In a monarchy, it is an excellent barrier to the despotism of the prince; in a republic, it is a no less excellent barrier to the encroachments and oppressions of the representative body. And it is the best expedient which can be devised in any government, to secure a steady, upright, and impartial administration of the laws.

Whoever attentively considers the different departments of

power must perceive, that, in a government in which they are separated from each other, the judiciary, from the nature of its functions, will always be the least dangerous to the political rights of the constitution; because it will be least in a capacity to annoy or injure them. The executive not only dispenses the honors, but holds the sword of the community: The legislature not only commands the purse, but prescribes the rules by which the duties and rights of every citizen are to be regulated: The judiciary, on the contrary, has no influence over either the sword or the purse; no direction either of the strength or of the wealth of the society; and can take no active resolution whatever. It may truly be said to have neither FORCE nor WILL, but merely judgment; and must ultimately depend upon the aid of the executive arm for the efficacious exercise even of this faculty.

This simple view of the matter suggests several important consequences: it proves incontestibly, that the judiciary is beyond comparison, the weakest of the three departments of power, that it can never attack with success either of the other two; and that all possible care is requisite to enable it to defend itself against their attacks. It equally proves, that, though individual oppression may now and then proceed from the courts of justice, the general liberty of the people can never be endangered from that quarter: I mean so long as the judiciary remains truly distinct from both the legislature and executive. For I agree, that "there is no liberty, if the power of judging be not separated from the legislative and executive powers." It proves, in the last place, that as liberty can have nothing to fear from the judiciary alone, but would have everything to fear from its union with either of the other departments; that, as all the effects of such an union must ensue from a dependence of the former on the latter, notwithstanding a nominal and apparent separation; that as, from the natural feebleness of the judiciary, it is in continual jeopardy of being overpowered, awed or influenced by its co-ordinate branches; that, as nothing can contribute so much to its firmness and independence as PERMANENCY IN OFFICE, this quality may therefore be justly regarded as an indispensable ingredient in its constitution; and, in a great measure, as the CITADEL of the public justice and the public security.

The complete independence of the courts of justice is peculiarly essential in a limited constitution. By a limited constitution, I understand one which contains certain specified exceptions to the legislative authority; such, for instance, as that it shall pass no bills of attainder, no *ex post facto* laws, and the like. Limitations of this kind can be preserved in practice no other way than through the medium of the courts of justice; whose duty it must be to declare all acts contrary to the manifest tenor of the constitution void. Without this, all the reservations of particular rights or privileges would amount to nothing.

Some perplexity respecting the right of the courts to pronounce legislative acts void, because contrary to the constitution, has arisen from an imagination that the doctrine would imply a superiority of the judiciary to the legislative power. It is urged that the authority which can declare the acts of another void, must necessarily be superior to the one whose acts may be declared void. As this doctrine is of great importance in all the American constitutions, a brief discussion of the grounds on which it rests cannot be unacceptable.

There is no position which depends on clearer principles than that every act of a delegated authority, contrary to the tenor of the commission under which it is exercised, is void. No legislative act, therefore, contrary to the constitution, can be valid. To deny this would be to affirm, that the deputy is greater than his principal; that the servant is above his master; that the representatives of the people are superior to the people themselves; that men, acting by virtue of powers, may do not only what their powers do not authorize, but what they forbid.

If it be said that the legislative body are themselves the constitutional judges of their own powers, and that the construction they put upon them is conclusive upon the other departments, it may be answered, that this cannot be the natural presumption, where it is not to be collected from any particular provisions in the constitution. It is not otherwise to be supposed that the constitution could intend to enable the representatives of the people to substitute their *will* to that of their constituents. It is far more rational to suppose that the courts were designed to be an intermediate body between the people and the legislature, in order, among other things, to keep the latter within the limits assigned to their authority. The interpretation of the laws is the proper and peculiar province of the courts. A constitution is, in fact, and must be, regarded by the judges as a fundamental law. It must therefore belong to them to ascertain its meaning, as well as the meaning of any particular act proceeding from the legislative body. If there should happen to be an irreconcilable variance between the two, that which has the superior obligation and validity ought, of course, to be preferred; in other words, the constitution ought to be preferred to the statute, the intention of the people to the intention of their agents.

Nor does the conclusion by any means suppose a superiority of the judicial to the legislative power. It only supposes that the power of the people is superior to both; and that where the will of the legislature declared in its statutes, stands in opposition to that of the people declared in the constitution, the judges ought to be governed by the latter, rather than the former. They ought to regulate their decisions by the fundamental laws, rather than by those which are not fundamental.

This exercise of judicial discretion, in determining between two contradictory laws, is exemplified in a familiar instance. It not uncommonly happens, that there are two statutes existing at one time, clashing in whole or in part with each other, and neither of them containing any repealing clause or expression. In such a case, it is the province of the courts to liquidate and fix their meaning and operation: So far as they can, by any fair construction be reconciled to each other, reason and law conspire to dictate that this should be done: Where this is impracticable, it becomes a matter of necessity to give effect to one, in exclusion of the other. The rule which has obtained in the courts for determining their relative validity is, that the last in order of time shall be preferred to the first. But this is a mere rule of construction, not derived from any positive law, but from the nature and reason of the thing. It is a rule not enjoined upon the courts by legislative provision, but adopted by themselves, as consonant to truth and propriety, for the direction of their conduct as interpreters of the law. They thought it reasonable, that between the interfering acts of an *equal* authority, that which was the last indication of its will should have the preference.

But in regard to the interfering acts of a superior and subordinate authority, of an original and derivative power, the nature and reason of the thing indicate the converse of that rule as proper to be followed. They teach us, that the prior act of a superior ought to be preferred to the subsequent act of an inferior and subordinate authority; and that, accordingly, whenever a particular statute contravenes the constitution, it will be the duty of the judicial tribunals to adhere to the latter, and disregard the former.

It can be of no weight to say, that the courts, on the pretense of a repugnancy, may substitute their own pleasure to the constitutional intentions of the legislature. This might as well happen in the case of two contradictory statutes; or it might as well happen in every adjudication upon any single statute. The courts must declare the sense of the law; and if they should be disposed to exercise WILL instead of JUDGMENT, the consequence would equally be the substitution of their pleasure to that of the legislative body. The observation, if it proved anything, would prove that there ought to be no judges distinct from that body.

If then the courts of justice are to be considered as the bulwarks of a limited constitution, against legislative encroachments, this consideration will afford a strong argument for the permanent tenure of judicial offices, since nothing will contribute so much as this to that independent spirit in the judges, which must be essential to the faithful performance of so arduous a duty.

This independence of the judges is equally requisite to guard the constitution and the rights of individuals, from the effects of those ill-humors which the arts of designing men, or the influence of particular conjunctures, sometimes disseminate among the people themselves, and which, though they speedily give place to better information, and more deliberate reflection, have a tendency, in the meantime, to occasion dangerous innovations in the government, and serious oppressions of the minor party in the community. Though I trust the friends of the proposed constitution will never concur with its enemies, in questioning that fundamental principle of republican government, which admits the right of the people to alter or abolish the established constitution whenever they find it inconsistent with their happiness; yet it is not to be inferred from this principle that the representatives of the people, whenever a momentary inclination happens to lay hold of a majority of their constituents incompatible with the provisions in the existing constitution, would, on that account, be justifiable in a violation of those provisions; or that the courts would be under a greater obligation to connive at infractions in this shape, than when they had proceeded wholly from the cabals of the representative body. Until the people have, by some solemn and authoritative act, annulled or changed the established form, it is binding upon themselves collectively, as well as individually; and no presumption, or even knowledge of their sentiments, can warrant their representatives in a departure from it, prior to such an act. But it is easy to see, that it would require an uncommon portion of fortitude in the judges to do their duty as faithful guardians of the constitution, where legislative invasions of it had been instigated by the major voice of the community.

But it is not with a view to infractions of the constitution only, that the independence of the judges may be an essential safeguard against the effects of occasional ill-humors in the society. These sometimes extend no farther than to the injury of the private rights of particular classes of citizens, by unjust and partial laws. Here also the firmness of the judicial magistracy is of vast importance in mitigating the severity, and confining the operation of such laws. It not only serves to moderate the immediate mischiefs of those which may have been passed, but it operates as a check upon the legislative body in passing them; who, perceiving that obstacles to the success of an iniquitous intention are to be expected from the scruples of the courts, are in a manner compelled by the very motives of the injustice they meditate, to qualify their attempts. This is a circumstance calculated to have more influence upon the character of our governments than but few may imagine. The benefits of the integrity and moderation of the judiciary have already been felt in more states than one; and though they may have displeased those whose sinister expectations they may have disappointed, they must have commanded the esteem and applause of all the virtuous and disinterested. Considerate men, of every description, ought to prize whatever will tend to beget or fortify that temper in the courts; as no man can be sure that he may not be tomorrow the victim of a spirit of injustice, by which he may be a gainer today. And every man must now feel that the inevitable tendency of such a spirit is to sap the foundations of public and private confidence, and to introduce in its stead universal distrust and distress.

That inflexible and uniform adherence to the rights of the constitution, and of individuals, which we perceive to be indispensable in the courts of justice, can certainly not be expected from judges who hold their offices by a temporary commission. Periodical appointments, however regulated, or by whomsoever made, would, in some way or other, be fatal to their necessary independence. If the power of making them was committed either to the executive or legislature, there would be danger of an improper complaisance to the branch which possessed it: if to both, there would be an unwillingness to hazard the displeasure of either; if to the people, or to persons chosen by them for the special purpose, there would be too great a disposition to consult popularity, to justify a reliance that nothing would be consulted but the constitution and the laws.

There is yet a further and a weighty reason for the permanency of judicial offices; which is deducible from the nature of the qualifications they require. It has been frequently remarked, with great propriety, that a voluminous code of laws is one of the inconveniences necessarily connected with the advantages of a free government. To avoid an arbitrary discretion in the courts, it is indispensable that they should be bound down by strict rules and precedents, which serve to define and point out their duty in every particular case that comes before them; and it will readily be conceived, from the variety of controversies which grow out of the folly and wickedness of mankind, that the records of those precedents must unavoidably swell to a very considerable bulk, and must demand long and laborious study to acquire a competent knowledge of them. Hence it is, that there can be but few men in the society, who will have sufficient skill in the laws to qualify them for the stations of judges. And making the proper deductions for the ordinary depravity of human nature, the number must be still smaller, of those who unite the requisite integrity with the requisite knowledge. These considerations apprise us, that the government can have no great option between fit characters; and that a temporary duration in office, which would naturally discourage such characters from quitting a lucrative line of practice to accept a seat on the bench, would have a tendency to throw the administration of justice into hands less able, and less well qualified, to conduct it with utility and dignity. In the present circumstances of this country, and in those in which it is likely to be for a long time to come, the disadvantages on this score would be greater than they may at first sight appear; but it must be confessed, that they are far inferior to those which present themselves under the other aspects of the subject.

Upon the whole, there can be no room to doubt, that the convention acted wisely in copying from the models of those constitutions which have established *good behavior* as the tenure of judicial offices, in point of duration; and that, so far from being blameable on this account, their plan would have been inexcusably defective, if it had wanted this important feature of good government. The experience of Great Britain affords an illustrious comment on the excellence of the institution.

Publius.

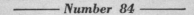 *Number 84* ————

Alexander Hamilton

Is a Bill of Rights Needed?

In the course of the foregoing review of the constitution, I had endeavored to answer most of the objections which have appeared against it. There remain, however, a few which either did not fall naturally under any particular head, or were forgotten in their proper places. These shall now be discussed: but as the subject has been drawn into great length, I shall so far consult brevity, as to comprise all my observations on these miscellaneous points in a single paper.

The most considerable of the remaining objections is, that the plan of the convention contains no bill of rights. Among other answers given to this, it has been upon different occasions remarked, that the constitutions of several of the states are in a similar predicament. I add, that New York is of the number. And yet the persons who in this state oppose the new system, while they profess an unlimited admiration for our particular constitution, are among the most intemperate partisans of a bill of rights. To justify their zeal in this matter they allege two things: one is, that though the constitution of New York has no bill of rights prefixed to it, yet it contains, in the body of it, various provisions in favor of particular privileges and rights, which, in substance, amount to the same thing; the other is, that the constitution adopts, in their full extent, the common and statute law of Great Britain, by which many other rights, not expressed, are equally secured.

To the first I answer, that the constitution offered by the convention contains, as well as the constitution of this state, a number of such provisions.

Independent of those which relate to the structure of the government, we find the following: Article I, section 3, clause 7. "Judgment in cases of impeachment shall not extend further than to removal from office, and disqualification to hold and enjoy any office of honor, trust, or profit under the United States; but the party convicted shall, nevertheless, be liable and subject to indictment, trial, judgment, and punishment, according to law." Section 9 of the same article, clause 2. "The privilege of the writ of *habeas corpus* shall not be suspended, unless when in cases of rebellion or invasion the public safety may require it." Clause 3. "No bill of attainder or *ex post facto* law shall be passed." Clause 7. "No title of nobility shall be granted by the United States; and no person holding any office of profit or trust under them, shall, without the consent of the congress, accept of any present, emolument, office, or title, of any kind whatever, from any king, prince, or foreign state." Article III, section 2, clause 3. "The trial of all crimes, except in cases of impeachment, shall be by jury; and such trial shall be held in the state where the said crimes shall have been committed; but when not committed within any state, the trial shall be at such place or places as the congress may by law have directed." Section 3 of the same article. "Treason against the United States shall consist only in levying war against them, or in adhering to their enemies, giving them aid and comfort. No person shall be convicted of treason, unless on the testimony of two witnesses to the same overt act, or on confession in open court." And clause 3 of the same section. "The congress shall have power to declare the punishment of treason; but no attainder of treason shall work corruption of blood, or forfeiture, except during the life of the person attained."

It may well be a question, whether these are not, upon the whole, of equal importance with any which are to be found in the constitution of this state. The establishment of the writ of *habeas corpus*, the prohibition of *ex post facto* laws, and of

TITLES OF NOBILITY, *to which we have no corresponding pro-*
visions in our constitution, are perhaps greater securities to
liberty than any it contains. The creation of crimes after the
commission of the fact, or, in other words, the subjecting of
men to punishment for things which, when they are done,
were breaches of no law; and the practice of arbitrary im-
prisonments have been, in all ages, the favorite and most
formidable instruments of tyranny. The observations of the
judicious Blackstone, in reference to the latter, are well worthy
of recital: "To bereave a man of life (says he) or by violence
to confiscate his estate, without accusation or trial, would
be so gross and notorious an act of despotism, as must at once
convey the alarm of tyranny throughout the whole nation; but
confinement of the person, by secretly hurrying him to jail,
where his sufferings are unknown or forgotten, is a less public,
a less striking, and therefore *a more dangerous engine* of arbitrary government." And as a remedy for this fatal evil, he is
everywhere peculiarly emphatical in his encomiums on the
habeas corpus act, which in one place he calls "the BULWARK
of the British constitution."

Nothing need be said to illustrate the importance of the
prohibition of titles of nobility. This may truly be denomi-
nated the cornerstone of republican government; for so long
as they are excluded, there can never be serious danger that
the government will be any other than that of the people.

To the second, that is, to the pretended establishment of
the common and statute law by the constitution, I answer, that
they are expressly made subject "to such alterations and provisions as the legislature shall from time to time make concerning the same." They are therefore at any moment liable
to repeal by the ordinary legislative power, and of course have
no constitutional sanction. The only use of the declaration was
to recognize the ancient law, and to remove doubts which
might have been occasioned by the revolution. This consequently can be considered as no part of a declaration of rights;
which under our constitutions must be intended to limit the
power of the government itself.

It has been several times truly remarked, that bills of rights are, in their origin, stipulations between kings and their subjects, abridgments of prerogative in favor of privilege, reservations of rights not surrendered to the prince. Such was MAGNA CHARTA, obtained by the Barons, sword in hand, from King John. Such were the subsequent confirmations of that charter by succeeding princes. Such was the *petition of right* assented to by Charles the First, in the beginning of his reign. Such also, was the declaration of right presented by the lords and commons to the Prince of Orange in 1688, and afterward thrown into the form of an act of parliament, called the bill of rights. It is evident, therefore, that according to their primitive signification, they have no application to constitutions professedly founded upon the power of the people, and executed by their immediate representatives and servants. Here, in strictness, the people surrender nothing; and as they retain everything, they have no need of particular reservations. "WE THE PEOPLE of the United States, to secure the blessings of liberty to ourselves and our posterity do *ordain* and *establish* this constitution for the United States of America"; This is a better recognition of popular rights, than volumes of those aphorisms, which make the principal figure in several of our state bills of rights, and which would sound much better in a treatise of ethics, than in a constitution of government.

But a minute detail of particular rights is certainly far less applicable to a constitution like that under consideration, which is merely intended to regulate the general political interests of the nation, than to one which has the regulation of every species of personal and private concerns. If therefore the loud clamors against the plan of the convention, on this score, are well founded, no epithets of reprobation will be too strong for the constitution of this state. But the truth is, that both of them contain all which, in relation to their objects, is reasonably to be desired.

I go further, and affirm, that bills of rights, in the sense and to the extent they are contended for, are not only unnecessary in the proposed constitution, but would even be dangerous. They would contain various exceptions to powers not granted, and on this very account would afford a colorable pretext to claim more than were granted. For why declare that things shall not be done which there is no power to do? Why, for instance, should it be said, that the liberty of the press shall not be restrained, when no power is given by which restrictions may be imposed? I will not contend that such a provision would confer a regulating power; but it is evident that it would furnish, to men disposed to usurp, a plausible pretense for claiming that power. They might urge with a semblance of reason that the constitution ought not to be charged with the absurdity of providing against the abuse of an authority, which was not given, and that the provision against restraining the liberty of the press afforded a clear implication, that a right to prescribe proper regulations concerning it, was intended to be vested in the national government. This may serve as a specimen of the numerous handles which would be given to the doctrine of constructive powers, by the indulgence of an injudicious zeal for bills of rights.

On the subject of the liberty of the press, as much has been said, I cannot forbear adding a remark or two: In the first place, I observe that there is not a syllable concerning it in the constitution of this state; in the next, I contend that whatever has been said about it in that of any other state, amounts to nothing. What signifies a declaration, that "the liberty of the press shall be inviolably preserved?" What is the liberty of the press? Who can give it any definition which would not leave the utmost latitude for evasion? I hold it to be impracticable; and from this I infer, that its security, whatever fine declarations may be inserted in any constitution respecting it, must altogether depend on public opinion, and on the general spirit of the people and of the government. And here, after all, as intimated upon another occasion, must we seek for the only solid basis of all our rights.

There remains but one other view of this matter to conclude the point. The truth is, after all the declamation we have heard, that the constitution is itself, in every rational sense, and to every useful purpose, A BILL OF RIGHTS. The several bills of rights, in Great Britain, form its constitution, and conversely the constitution of each state is its bill of rights. In like manner the proposed constitution, if adopted, will be the bill of rights of the union. Is it one object of a bill of rights to declare and specify the political privileges of the citizens in the structure and administration of the government? This is done in the most ample and precise manner in the plan of the convention; comprehending various precautions for the public security, which are not to be found in any of the state constitutions. Is another object of a bill of rights to define certain immunities and modes of proceeding, which are relative to personal and private concerns? This we have seen has also been attended to, in a variety of cases, in the same plan. Adverting therefore to the substantial meaning of a bill of rights, it is absurd to allege that it is not to be found in the work of the convention. It may be said that it does not go far enough, though it will not be easy to make this appear; but it can with no propriety be contended that there is no such thing. It certainly must be immaterial what mode is observed as to the order of declaring the rights of the citizens, if they are provided for in any part of the instrument which establishes the government. Whence it must be apparent that much of what has been said on this subject rests merely on verbal and nominal distinctions, entirely foreign to the substance of the thing.

Another objection, which, from the frequency of its repetition, may be presumed to be relied on, is of this nature: It is improper (say the objectors) to confer such large powers, as are proposed, upon the national government: because the seat of that government must of necessity be too remote from many of the states to admit of a proper knowledge on the part of the constituent, of the conduct of the representative body. This argument, if it proves anything, proves that there ought to be no general government whatever. For the powers which it seems to be agreed on all hands, ought to be vested in the union, cannot be safely entrusted to a body which is not under every requisite control. But there are satisfactory reasons to show that the objection is, in reality, not well founded. There is in most of the arguments which relate to distance, a palpable illusion of the imagination. What are the sources of information, by which the people in any distant county must regulate their judgment of the conduct of their representatives in the state legislature? Of personal observation they can have no benefit. This is confined to the citizens on the spot. They must therefore depend on the formation of intelligent men, in whom they confide: and how must these men obtain their information? Evidently from the complexion of public measures, from the public prints, from correspondences with their representatives, and with other persons who reside at the place of their deliberations.

It is equally evident that the like sources of information would be open to the people, in relation to the conduct of their representatives in the general government; and the impediments to a prompt communication which distance may be supposed to create, will be overbalanced by the effects of the vigilance of the state governments. The executive and legislative bodies of each state will be so many sentinels over the persons employed in every department of the national administration; and as it will be in their power to adopt and pursue a regular and effectual system of intelligence, they can never be at a loss to know the behavior of those who represent their constituents in the national councils, and can readily communicate the same knowledge to the people. Their disposition to apprise the community of whatever may prejudice its interests from another quarter, may be relied upon, if it were only from the rivalship of power. And we may conclude with the fullest assurance, that the people, through that channel, will be better informed of the conduct of their national representatives, than they can be by any means they now possess, of that of their state representatives.

It ought also to be remembered, that the citizens who inhabit the country at and near the seat of government will, in all questions that affect the general liberty and prosperity, have the same interest with those who are at a distance; and that they will stand ready to sound the alarm when necessary, and to point out the actors in any pernicious project. The pub-

1) Introduction - Judge fairly
   & impartially - do not be
   swayed by others -

10) Factions - causes & effect -
    Cause is freedom
    effects must be controlled!
Democracy v Republic -

47) Separation of Power -
    Quotes Montesquieu
    Shows how state constitutions
    are similar to US Constitution
Branches Separated but overlap duties
N.J. Most blended   N.H. best
resemblance of U.S Constitution
Madison wanted to show that
the change + did not violating the sacred
maxim of free gov't was not
warranted - (TO BE CON'T)

51) Each department should have
as little agency as possible
in the appointment of members of
other departments

Gov't must control the governed &
then control itself - the People control
the government

Justice is the End of Government

Returns to theory of factions to
prove need for Federal Gov. & -

78) Supreme Court - no argument
against the need for it, just
the manner of constituting it
& its extent - How do you
appoint Judges - Tenure - & division
of the courts authority among itself

P₅ 143

least attack other departments. Weakest
department - must be absolutely free
of dependence & separated from other
2 departments - Constitution is
a fundamental Law & Judges must
interpret it -

26) Supreme Court (Cont)

Tenure is determined by
good behavior -

Law is so voluminous as
to necessitate long terms of
office or life-

pluralism — a society
broken into many groups &
interest, all of which pursue
their separate goals —
Type of class struggle

Gov't job: regulation of &
refereeing these warring groups
This is the principal task
of modern legislation
    Its standpoint must be
the common good or welfare

———————

Fractionalism — kind of pluralism
is good in that a minority
can never be dominated since
it takes many minors to make
a majority — Each group pursues its
own goals & protect minority
    freedom.

lic papers will be expeditious messengers of intelligence to the most remote inhabitants of the union.

Among the many curious objections which have appeared against the proposed constitution, the most extraordinary and the least colorable is derived from the want of some provision respecting the debts *due* to the United States. This has been represented as a tacit relinquishment of those debts, and as a wicked contrivance to screen public defaulters. The newspapers have teemed with the most inflammatory railings on this head; yet there is nothing clearer than that the suggestion is entirely void of foundation, the offspring of extreme ignorance or extreme dishonesty. In addition to the remarks I have made upon the subject in another place, I shall only observe, that as it is a plain dictate of common sense, so it is also an established doctrine of political law, that "*States neither lose any of their rights, nor are discharged from any of their obligations, by a change in the form of their civil government.*"

The last objection of any consequence at present recollected, turns upon the article of expense. If it were even true, that the adoption of the proposed government would occasion a considerable increase of expense, it would be an objection that ought to have no weight against the plan. The great bulk of the citizens of America are with reason convinced that union is the basis of their political happiness. Men of sense of all parties now, with few exceptions, agree that it cannot be preserved under the present system, nor without radical alterations; that new and extensive powers ought to be granted to the national head, and that these require a different organization of the federal government; a single body being an unsafe depository of such ample authorities. In conceding all this, the question of expense is given up; for it is impossible, with any degree of safety, to narrow the foundation upon which the system is to stand. The two branches of the legislature are, in the first instance, to consist of only sixty-five persons; the same number of which congress, under the existing confederation, may be composed. It is true that this number is intended to be increased; but this is to keep pace with the progress of the population and resources of the country. It is evident that a less number would, even in the first instance, have been unsafe; and that a continuance of the present number would, in a more advanced stage of population, be a very inadequate representation of the people.

Whence is the dreaded augmentation of expense to spring? One source indicated, is the multiplication of offices under the new government. Let us examine this a little.

It is evident that the principal departments of the administration under the present government, are the same which will be required under the new. There are now a secretary of war, a secretary for foreign affairs, a secretary for domestic affairs, a board of treasury consisting of three persons, a treasurer, assistants, clerks, etc. These offices are indispensable under any system, and will suffice under the new, as well as the old. As to ambassadors and other ministers and agents in foreign countries, the proposed constitution can make no other difference, than to render their characters, where they reside, more respectable, and their services more useful. As to persons to be employed in the collection of the revenues, it is unquestionably true that these will form a very considerable addition to the number of federal officers; but it will not follow that this will occasion an increase of public expense. It will be in most cases nothing more than an exchange of state for national officers. In the collection of all duties, for instance, the persons employed will be wholly of the latter description. The states individually, will stand in no need of any for this purpose. What difference can it make in point of expense, to pay officers of the customs appointed by the state, or by the United States?

Where, then, are we to seek for those additional articles of expense, which are to swell the account to the enormous size that has been represented? The chief item which occurs to me, respects the support of the judges of the United States. I do not add the president, because there is now a president of congress, whose expenses may not be far, if anything, short of those which will be incurred on account of the president of the United States. The support of the judges will clearly be an extra expense, but to what extent will depend on the particular plan which may be adopted in regard to this matter. But upon no reasonable plan can it mount to a sum which will be an object of material consequence.

Let us now see what there is to counterbalance any extra expense that may attend the establishment of the proposed government. The first thing which presents itself is, that a great part of the business, that now keeps congress sitting through the year, will be transacted by the president. Even the management of foreign negotiations will naturally devolve upon him according to general principles concerted with the senate, and subject to their final concurrence. Hence it is evident, that a portion of the year will suffice for the session of both the senate and the house of representatives: We may suppose about a fourth for the latter, and a third, or perhaps half, for the former. The extra business of treaties and appointments may give this extra occupation to the senate. From this circumstance we may infer, that until the house of representatives shall be increased greatly beyond its present number, there will be a considerable saving of expense from the difference between the constant session of the present, and the temporary session of the future congress.

But there is another circumstance, of great importance in the view of economy. The business of the United States has hitherto occupied the state legislatures, as well as congress. The latter has made requisitions which the former have had to provide for. It has thence happened, that the sessions of the state legislatures have been protracted greatly beyond what was necessary for the execution of the mere local business. More than half their time has been frequently employed in matters which related to the United States. Now the members who compose the legislatures of the several states amount to two thousand and upward; which number has hitherto performed what, under the new system, will be done in the first instance by sixty-five persons, and probably at no future period by above a fourth or a fifth of that number. The congress under the proposed government will do all the business of the United States themselves, without the intervention of the state legislatures, who thenceforth will have only to attend to the affairs of their particular states, and will not have to sit in any proportion as long as they have heretofore done. This difference, in the time of the sessions of the state legislatures, will be clear gain, and will alone form an article of saving, which may be regarded as an equivalent for any additional objects of expense that may be occasioned by the adoption of the new system.

The result from these observations is, that the sources of additional expense from the establishment of the proposed constitution are much fewer than may have been imagined; that they are counterbalanced by considerable objects of saving; and that, while it is questionable on which side the scale will preponderate, it is certain that a government less expensive would be incompetent to the purposes of the union.

PUBLIUS.

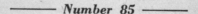

——— *Number 85* ———

Alexander Hamilton

Conclusion: A National Government for a New Nation.

According to the formal division of the subject of these papers, announced in my first number, there would appear still to remain for discussion two points—"the analogy of the proposed government to your own state constitution," and "the additional security which its adoption will afford to republican government, to liberty, and to property." But these heads have been so fully anticipated, and so completely exhausted in the progress of the work, that it would now scarcely be possible to do anything more than repeat, in a more dilated form, what has been already said; which the advanced stage of the question, and the time already spent upon it, con-spire to forbid.

It is remarkable, that the resemblance of the plan of the convention to the act which organizes the government of this state holds, not less with regard to many of the supposed de-fects, than to the real excellencies of the former. Among the pretended defects are the re-eligibility of the executive; the want of a council; the omission of a formal bill of rights; the omission of a provision respecting the liberty of the press: These, and several others, which have been noted in the course of our inquiries, are as much chargeable on the exist-ing constitution of this state, as on the one proposed for the Union: and a man must have slender pretensions to consist-ency, who can rail at the latter for imperfections which he finds no difficulty in excusing in the former. Nor indeed can there be a better proof of the insincerity and affectation of some of the zealous adversaries of the plan of the convention, who profess to be devoted admirers of the government of this state, than the fury with which they have attacked that plan, for matters in regard to which our own constitution is equally, or perhaps more vulnerable.

The additional securities to republican government, to liber-ty and to property, to be derived from the adoption of the plan, consist chiefly in the restraints which the preservation of the union will impose upon local factions and insurrections, and upon the ambition of powerful individuals in single states, who might acquire credit and influence enough, from leaders and favorites, to become the despots of the people; in the di-minution of the opportunities to foreign intrigue, which the dissolution of the confederacy would invite and facilitate; in the prevention of extensive military establishments, which could not fail to grow out of wars between the states in a disunited situation; in the express guarantee of a republican form of government to each; in the absolute and universal ex-clusion of titles of nobility; and in the precautions against the repetition of those practices on the part of the state govern-ments, which have undermined the foundations of property and credit; have planted mutual distrust in the breasts of all classes of citizens; and have occasioned an almost universal prostration of morals.

Thus have I, fellow-citizens, executed the task I had assigned to myself; with what success your conduct must determine. I trust, at least, you will admit that I have not failed in the assurance I gave you respecting the spirit with which my endeavors should be conducted. I have addressed myself purely to your judgments, and have studiously avoided those asperities which are too apt to disgrace political disputants of all parties, and which have been not a little provoked by the language and conduct of the opponents of the constitution. The charge of a conspiracy against the liberties of the people, which has been indiscriminately brought against the advocates of the plan, has something in it too wanton and too malignant not to excite the indignation of every man who feels in his own bosom a refutation of the calumny. The perpetual changes which have been rung upon the wealthy, the well-born, and the great, are such as to inspire the disgust of all sensible men. And the unwarrantable concealments and misrepresentations, which have been in various ways practiced to keep the truth from the public eye, are of a nature to demand the reprobation of all honest men. It is possible that these circumstances may have occasionally betrayed me into intemperances of expression which I did not intend: It is certain that I have frequently felt a struggle between sensibility and moderation; and if the former has in some instances prevailed, it must be my excuse, that it has been neither often nor much.

Let us now pause, and ask ourselves whether, in the course of these papers, the proposed constitution has not been satisfactorily vindicated from the aspersions thrown upon it; and whether it has not been shown to be worthy of the public approbation, and necessary to the public safety and prosperity. Every man is bound to answer these questions to himself, according to the best of his conscience and understanding, and to act agreeably to the genuine and sober dictates of his judgment. This is a duty from which nothing can give him a dispensation. It is one that he is called upon, nay, constrained by all the obligations that form the bands of society, to discharge sincerely and honestly. No partial motive, no particular interest, no pride of opinion, no temporary passion or prejudice, will justify to himself, to his country, to his posterity, an improper election of the part he is to act. Let him beware of an obstinate adherence to party: Let him reflect, that the object upon which he is to decide is not a particular interest of the community, but the very existence of the nation: And let him remember, that a majority of America has already given its sanction to the plan which he is to approve or reject.

I shall not dissemble that I feel an entire confidence in the arguments which recommend the proposed system to your adoption; and that I am unable to discern any real force in those by which it has been assailed. I am persuaded that it is the best which our political situation, habits, and opinions will admit, and superior to any the revolution has produced.

Concessions on the part of the friends of the plan that it has not a claim to absolute perfection, have afforded matter of no small triumph to its enemies. Why, say they, should we adopt an imperfect thing? Why not amend it, and make it perfect before it is irrevocably established? This may be plausible, but it is plausible only. In the first place I remark that the extent of these concessions has been greatly exaggerated. They have been stated as amounting to an admission that the plan is radically defective; and that, without material alterations, the rights and the interests of the community cannot be safely confided to it. This, as far as I have understood the meaning of those who make the concessions, is an entire perversion of their sense. No advocate of the measure can be found who will not declare as his sentiment, that the system, though it may not be perfect in every part, is, upon the whole, a good one; is the best that the present views and circumstances of the country will permit; and is such an one as promises every species of security which a reasonable people can desire.

I answer in the next place, that I should esteem it the extreme of imprudence to prolong the precarious state of our national affairs, and to expose the union to the jeopardy of successive experiments, in the chimerical pursuit of a perfect plan. I never expect to see a perfect work from imperfect man. The result of the deliberations of all collective bodies, must necessarily be a compound as well of the errors and prejudices, as of the good sense and wisdom of the individuals of whom they are composed. The compacts which are to embrace thirteen distinct states, in a common bond of amity and union, must as necessarily be a compromise of as many dissimilar interests and inclinations. How can perfection spring from such materials?

The reasons assigned in an excellent little pamphlet lately published in this city, unanswerably show the utter improbability of assembling a new convention, under circumstances in any degree so favorable to a happy issue, as those in which the late convention met, deliberated, and concluded. I will not repeat the arguments there used, as I presume the production itself has had an extensive circulation. It is, certainly well worth the perusal of every friend to his country. There is, however, one point of light in which the subject of amendments still remains to be considered; and in which it has not yet been exhibited. I cannot resolve to conclude without first taking a survey of it in this aspect.

It appears to me susceptible of complete demonstration, that it will be far more easy to obtain subsequent than previous amendments to the constitution. The moment an alteration is made in the present plan, it becomes, to the purpose of adoption, a new one, and must undergo a new decision of each state. To its complete establishment throughout the union, it will therefore require the concurrence of thirteen states. If, on the contrary, the constitution should once be ratified by all the states as it stands, alterations in it may at any time be effected by nine states. In this view alone the chances are as thirteen to nine in favor of subsequent amendments, rather than of the original adoption of an entire system.

This is not all. Every constitution for the United States must inevitably consist of a great variety of particulars, in which thirteen independent states are to be accommodated in their interests or opinions of interest. We may, of course, expect to see, in any body of men charged with its original formation, very different combinations of the parts upon different points. Many of those who form the majority on one question may become the minority on a second, and an association dissimilar to either, may constitute the majority on a third. Hence the necessity of molding and arranging all the particulars which are to compose the whole, in such a manner, as to satisfy all the parties to the compact; and hence also an immense multiplication of difficulties and casualties in obtaining the collective assent to a final act. The degree of that multiplication must evidently be in a ratio to the number of particulars and the number of parties.

But every amendment to the constitution, if once established, would be a single proposition, and might be brought forward singly. There would then be no necessity for management or compromise, in relation to any other point; no giving nor taking. The will of the requisite number would at once bring the matter to a decisive issue. And consequently whenever nine, or rather ten, states were united in the desire of a particular amendment, that amendment must infallibly prevail. There can, therefore, be no comparison between the facility of effecting an amendment, and that of establishing in the first instance a complete constitution.

In opposition to the probability of subsequent amendments it has been urged that the persons delegated to the administration of the national government, will always be disinclined to yield up any portion of the authority of which they were once possessed. For my own part, I acknowledge a thorough conviction that any amendments which may, upon mature consideration, be thought useful, will be applicable to the organization of the government, not to the mass of its powers; and on this account alone, I think there is no weight in the observation just stated. I also think there is little force in it on another account. The intrinsic difficulty of governing THIRTEEN STATES, independent of calculations upon an ordinary degree of public spirit and integrity, will, in my opinion, constantly *impose* on the national rulers, the *necessity* of a spirit of accommodation to the reasonable expectations of their constituents. But there is yet a further consideration, which proves beyond the possibility of doubt, that the observation is futile. It is this, that the national rulers, whenever nine states concur, will have no option upon the subject. By the fifth article of the plan the congress will be *obliged*, "on the application of the legislatures of two-thirds of the states, (which at present amount to nine) to call a convention for proposing amendments, which *shall be valid* to all intents and purposes, as part of the constitution, when ratified by the legislatures of three-fourths of the states, or by conventions in three-fourths thereof." The words of this article are peremptory. The congress *"shall* call a convention." Nothing in this particular is left to discretion. Of consequence all the declamation about the disinclination to a change vanishes in air. Nor, however difficult it may be supposed to unite two-thirds, or three-fourths, of the state legislatures, in amendments which may affect local interests, can there be any room to apprehend any such difficulty in a union on points which are merely relative to the general liberty or security of the people. We may safely rely on the disposition of the state legislatures to erect barriers against the encroachments of the national authority.

If the foregoing argument be a fallacy, certain it is that I am myself deceived by it; for it is, in my conception, one of those rare instances in which a political truth can be brought to the test of mathematical demonstration. Those who see the matter in the same light, however zealous they may be for amendments, must agree in the propriety of a previous adoption, as the most direct road to their object.

The zeal for attempts to amend, prior to the establishment of the constitution, must abate in every man, who is ready to accede to the truth of the following observations of a writer, equally solid and ingenious: "To balance a large state or society (says he) whether monarchical or republican, on general laws, is a work of so great difficulty, that no human genius, however comprehensive, is able by the mere dint of reason and reflection, to effect it. The judgments of many must unite in the work: EXPERIENCE must guide their labor: TIME must bring it to perfection: And the FEELING of inconveniences must correct the mistakes which they *inevitably* fall into, in their first trials and experiments." These judicious reflections contain a lesson of moderation to all the sincere lovers of the union, and ought to put them upon their guard against hazarding anarchy, civil war, a perpetual alienation of the states from each other, and perhaps the military despotism of a victorious demagogue, in the pursuit of what they are not likely to obtain, but from TIME and EXPERIENCE. It may be in me a defect of political fortitude, but I acknowledge that I cannot entertain an equal tranquillity with those who affect to treat the dangers of a longer continuance in our present situation as imaginary. A NATION without a NATIONAL GOVERNMENT is an awful spectacle. The establishment of a constitution, in time of profound peace, by the voluntary consent of a whole people, is a PRODIGY, to the completion of which I look forward with trembling anxiety. In so arduous an enterprise, I can reconcile it to no rules of prudence to let go the hold we now have, upon seven out of the thirteen states; and after having passed over so considerable a part of the ground, to recommence the course. I dread the more the consequences of new attempts, because I KNOW that POWERFUL INDIVIDUALS, in this and in other states, are enemies to a general national government in every possible shape.

PUBLIUS.

THE FEDERAL CONSTITUTION

BY THE CONVENTION,
SEPTEMBER 17, 1787

WE THE PEOPLE *of the United States, in order to form a more perfect Union, establish Justice, insure domestic Tranquillity, provide for the common Defence, promote the general Welfare, and secure the Blessings of Liberty to ourselves and our posterity, do ordain and establish this CONSTITUTION for the United States of America.*

ARTICLE I

SECTION 1. All legislative powers herein granted shall be vested in a congress of the United States, which shall consist of a senate and house of representatives.

SECTION 2. The house of representatives shall be composed of members chosen every second year by the people of the several states, and the electors in each state shall have the qualifications requisite for electors of the most numerous branch of the state legislature.

No person shall be a representative who shall not have attained to the age of twenty-five years, and been seven years a citizen of the United States, and who shall not, when elected, be an inhabitant of that state in which he shall be chosen.

Representatives and direct taxes shall be apportioned among the several states which may be included within this union, according to their respective numbers, which shall be determined by adding to the whole number of free persons, including those bound to service for a term of years, and excluding Indians not taxed, three-fifths of all other persons. The actual enumeration shall be made within three years after the first meeting of the congress of the United States, and within every subsequent term of ten years, in such manner as they shall by law direct. The number of representatives shall not exceed one for every thirty thousand, but each state shall have at least one representative; and until such enumeration shall be made, the state of New Hampshire shall be entitled to choose three, Massachusetts eight, Rhode Island and Providence Plantations one, Connecticut five, New York six, New Jersey four, Pennsylvania eight, Delaware one, Maryland six, Virginia ten, North Carolina five, South Carolina five, and Georgia three.

When vacancies happen in the representation from any state, the executive authority thereof shall issue writs of election to fill such vacancies.

The house of representatives shall choose their speaker and other officers; and shall have the sole power of impeachment.

SECTION 3. The senate of the United States shall be composed of two senators from each state, chosen by the legislature thereof, for six years; and each senator shall have one vote.

Immediately after they shall be assembled in consequence of the first election, they shall be divided as equally as may be into three classes. The seats of the senators of the first class shall be vacated at the expiration of the second year, the second class at the expiration of the fourth year, and the third class at the expiration of the sixth year, so that one-third may be chosen every second year; and if vacancies happen by resignation or otherwise, during the recess of the legislature of any state, the executive thereof may make temporary appointments until the next meeting of the legislature, which shall then fill such vacancies.

No person shall be a Senator who shall not have attained to the age of thirty years, and been nine years a citizen of the United States, and who shall not, when elected, be an inhabitant of that state for which he shall be chosen.

The vice-president of the United States shall be president of the senate, but shall have no vote, unless they be equally divided.

The senate shall choose their other officers, and also a president *pro tempore,* in the absence of the vice-president, or when he shall exercise the office of president of the United States.

The senate shall have the sole power to try all impeachments. When sitting for that purpose they shall be on oath or affirmation. When the president of the United States is tried, the chief justice shall preside. And no person shall be convicted without the concurrence of two-thirds of the members present.

Judgment in cases of impeachment shall not extend further than to removal from office, and disqualification to hold and enjoy any office of honour, trust, or profit, under the United States; but the party convicted shall, nevertheless, be liable and subject to indictment, trial, judgment, and punishment, according to law.

SECTION 4. The times, places, and manner of holding elections for senators and representatives, shall be prescribed in each state by the legislature thereof: but the congress may at any time by law make or alter such regulations, except as to the places of choosing senators.

The congress shall assemble at least once in every year, and such meeting shall be on the first Monday in December, unless they shall by law appoint a different day.

SECTION 5. Each house shall be the judge of the elections, returns, and qualifications of its own members; and a majority of each shall constitute a quorum to do business: but a smaller number may adjourn from day to day, and may be authorized to compel the attendance of absent members, in such manner, and under such penalties, as each house may provide.

Each house may determine the rules of its proceedings, punish its members for disorderly behaviour, and, with the concurrence of two-thirds, expel a member.

Each house shall keep a journal of its proceedings, and from time to time publish the same, excepting such parts as may in their judgment require secrecy; and the yeas and nays of the members of either house on any question shall, at the desire of one-fifth of those present, be entered on the journal.

Neither house, during the session of congress, shall, without the consent of the other, adjourn for more than three days, nor to any other place than that in which the two houses shall be sitting.

SECTION 6. The senators and representatives shall receive a compensation for their services, to be ascertained by law, and paid out of the treasury of the United States. They shall in all cases, except treason, felony, and breach of the peace, be privileged from arrest during their attendance at the session of their respective houses, and in going to and returning from the same, and for any speech or debate in either house, they shall not be questioned in any other place.

No senator or representative shall, during the time for which he was elected, be appointed to any civil office under the authority of the United States, which shall have been created, or the emoluments whereof shall have been increased during such time; and no person holding any office under the United States, shall be a member of either house during his continuance in office.

SECTION 7. All bills for raising revenue shall originate in the house of representatives; but the senate may propose or concur with amendments as on other bills.

Every bill which shall have passed the house of representatives and the senate shall, before it become a law, be presented to the president of the United States; if he approve, he shall sign it; but if not, he shall return it, with his objections, to that house in which it shall have originated, who shall enter the objections at large on their journal, and proceed to reconsider it. If after such reconsideration two-thirds of that house shall agree to pass the bill, it shall be sent, together with the objections, to the other house, by which it shall likewise be reconsidered, and if approved by two-thirds of that house, it shall become law. But in all such cases the votes of both houses shall be determined by yeas and nays, and the names of the persons voting for and against the bill shall be entered on the journal of each house respectively. If any bill shall not be returned by the president within ten days (Sundays excepted) after it shall have been presented to him, the same shall be a law, in like manner as if he had signed it, unless the congress by their adjournment prevent its return, in which case it shall not be a law.

Every order, resolution, or vote, to which the concurrence of the senate and house of representatives may be necessary (except on a question of adjournment) shall be presented to the president of the United States; and before the same shall take effect, shall be approved by him, or, being disapproved by him, shall be repassed by two-thirds of the senate and house of representatives, according to the rules and limitations prescribed in the case of a bill.

SECTION 8. The congress shall have power,

To lay and collect taxes, duties, imposts, and excises, to pay the debts and provide for the common defence and general welfare of the United States; but all duties, imposts, and excises, shall be uniform throughout the United States:

To borrow money on the credit of the United States:

To regulate commerce with foreign nations, and among the several states, and with the Indian tribes:

To establish an uniform rule of naturalization, and uniform laws on the subjects of bankruptcies throughout the United States:

To coin money, regulate the value thereof, and of foreign coin, and fix the standard of weights and measures:

To provide for the punishment of counterfeiting the securities and current coin of the United States:

To establish post-offices and post-roads:

To promote the progress of science and useful arts, by securing for limited times to authors and inventors the exclusive right to their respective writings and discoveries:

To constitute tribunals inferior to the supreme court:

To define and punish piracies and felonies committed on the high seas, and offences against the law of nations:

To declare war, grant letters of marque and reprisal, and make rules concerning captures on land and water:

To raise and support armies, but no appropriation of money to that use shall be for a longer term than two years:

To provide and maintain a navy:

To make rules for the government and regulation of the land and naval forces:

To provide for calling forth the militia to execute the laws of the union, suppress insurrections, and repel invasions:

To provide for organizing, arming, and disciplining the militia, and for governing such parts of them as may be employed in the service of the United States, reserving to the states respectively, the appointment of the officers, and the authority of training the militia according to the discipline prescribed by congress:

To exercise exclusive legislation in all cases whatsoever, over such district (not exceeding ten miles square) as may, by cession of particular states, and the acceptance of congress, become the seat of the government of the United States, and to exercise like authority over all places purchased by the consent of the legislature of the state in which the same shall be, for the erection of forts, magazines, arsenals, dockyards, and other needful buildings: And,

To make all laws which shall be necessary and proper for carrying into execution the foregoing powers, and all other powers vested by this constitution in the government of the United States, or in any department or officer thereof.

SECTION 9. The migration or importation of such persons as any of the states now existing shall think proper to admit, shall not be prohibited by the congress prior to the year one thousand eight hundred and eight, but a tax or duty may be imposed on such importation, not exceeding ten dollars for each person.

The privilege of the writ of *habeas corpus* shall not be suspended, unless when in cases of rebellion or invasion the public safety may require it.

No bill of attainder or *ex post facto* law shall be passed.

No capitation, or other direct tax shall be laid, unless in proportion to the *census* or enumeration herein before directed to be taken.

No tax or duty shall be laid on articles exported from any state. No preference shall be given by any regulation of commerce or revenue to the ports of one state over those of another; nor shall vessels bound to, or from, one state, be obliged to enter, clear, or pay duties in another.

No money shall be drawn from the treasury, but in consequence of appropriations made by law; and a regular statement and account of the receipts and expenditures of all public money shall be published from time to time.

No title of nobility shall be granted by the United States: And no person holding any office of profit or trust under them, shall, without the consent of the congress, accept of any present, emolument, office, or title, of any kind whatever, from any king, prince, or foreign state.

SECTION 10. No state shall enter into any treaty, alliance, or confederation; grant letters of marque, and reprisal; coin money; emit bills of credit; make anything but gold and silver coin a tender in payment of debts; pass any bill of attainder, *ex post facto* law, or law impairing the obligation of contracts; or grant any title of nobility.

No state shall, without the consent of the congress, lay any imposts or duties on imports or exports, except what may be absolutely necessary for executing its inspection laws; and the net proceeds of all duties and imposts, laid by any state on imports or exports, shall be for the use of the treasury of the United States; and all such laws shall be subject to the revision and control of the congress. No state shall, without the consent of congress, lay any duties of tonnage, keep troops, or ships of war, in time of peace, enter into any agreement or compact with another state, or with a foreign power, or engage in war, unless actually invaded, or in such imminent danger as will not admit of delay.

ARTICLE II

SECTION 1. The executive power shall be vested in a president of the United States of America. He shall hold his office during the term of four years, and together with the vice-president, chosen for the same term, be elected as follows:

Each state shall appoint, in such manner as the legislature thereof may direct, a number of electors, equal to the whole number of senators and representatives to which the state may be entitled in the congress: but no senator or representative, or person holding an office of trust or profit under the United States, shall be appointed an elector.

The electors shall meet in their respective states, and vote by ballot for two persons, of whom one at least shall not be an inhabitant of the same state with themselves. And they shall make a list of all the persons voted for, and of the number of votes for each; which list they shall sign and certify, and transmit sealed to the seat of the government of the United States, directed to the president of the senate. The president of the senate shall, in the presence of the senate and house of representatives, open all the certificates, and the votes shall then be counted. The person having the greatest number of votes shall be the president, if such number be a majority of the whole number of electors appointed; and if there be more than one who have such majority, and have an equal number of votes, then the house of representatives shall immediately choose by ballot one of them for president; and if no person have a majority, then from the five highest on the list the said house shall in like manner choose the president. But in choosing the president, the votes shall be taken by states, the representation from each state having one vote; a quorum for this purpose shall consist of a member or members from two-thirds of the states, and a majority of all the states shall be necessary to a choice. In every case, after the choice of the president, the person having the greatest number of votes of the electors shall be the vice-president. But if there should remain two or more who have equal votes, the senate shall choose from them by ballot the vice-president.

The congress may determine the time of choosing the electors, and the day on which they shall give their votes; which day shall be the same throughout the United States.

No person except a natural born citizen, or a citizen of the United States, at the time of the adoption of this constitution, shall be eligible to the office of president; neither shall any person be eligible to that office who shall not have attained to the age of thirty-five years, and been fourteen years a resident within the United States.

In case of removal of the president from office, or of his death, resignation, or inability to discharge the powers and duties of the said office, the same shall devolve on the vicepresident, and the congress may by law provide for the case of removal, death, resignation, or inability, both of the president and vice-president, declaring what officer shall then act as president, and such officer shall act accordingly, until the disability be removed, or a president shall be elected.

The president shall, at stated times, receive for his services a compensation, which shall neither be increased or diminished during the period for which he shall have been elected, and he shall not receive within that period any other emolument from the United States, or any of them.

Before he enter into the execution of his office, he shall take the following oath or affirmation:

'I do solemnly swear (or affirm) that I will faithfully execute the office of president of the United States, and will to the best of my ability, preserve, protect, and defend the constitution of the United States.'

SECTION 2. The president shall be commander in chief of the army and navy of the United States; and of the militia of the several states, when called into the actual service of the United States; he may require the opinion, in writing, of the principal officer in each of the executive departments, upon any subject relating to the duties of their respective offices, and he shall have power to grant reprieves and pardons for offences against the United States, except in cases of impeachment.

He shall have power, by and with the advice and consent of the senate, to make treaties, provided two-thirds of the senators present concur; and he shall nominate, and by and with the advice and consent of the senate, shall appoint ambassadors, other public ministers and consuls, judges of the supreme court, and all other officers of the United States, whose appointments are not herein otherwise provided for, and which shall be established by law. But the congress may by law vest the appointment of such inferior officers, as they think proper, in the president alone, in the courts of law, or in the heads of departments.

The president shall have power to fill up all vacancies that may happen during the recess of the senate, by granting commissions which shall expire at the end of their next session.

SECTION 3. He shall from time to time give to the congress information of the state of the union, and recommend to their consideration such measures as he shall judge necessary and expedient; he may, on extraordinary occasions, convene both houses, or either of them, and in case of disagreement between them, with respect to the time of adjournment, he may adjourn them to such time as he shall think proper; he shall receive ambassadors and other public ministers; he shall take care that the laws be faithfully executed, and shall commission all the officers of the United States.

SECTION 4. The president, vice-president, and all civil officers of the United States shall be removed from office on impeachment for, and conviction of, treason, bribery, or other high crimes and misdemeanours.

ARTICLE III

SECTION 1. The judicial power of the United States shall be vested in one supreme court, and in such inferior courts as the congress may from time to time ordain and establish. The judges, both of the supreme and inferior courts, shall hold their offices during good behaviour, and shall at stated times, receive for their services a compensation, which shall not be diminished during their continuance in office.

SECTION 2. The judicial power shall extend to all cases in law and equity, arising under this constitution, the laws of the United States, and treaties made, or which shall be made, under their authority; to all cases affecting ambassadors, other public ministers and consuls; to all cases of admiralty and maritime jurisdiction; to controversies to which the United States shall be a party; to controversies between two or more states; between a state and citizens of another state; between

now Pres. makes almost all laws.

citizens of different states; between citizens of the same state claiming lands under grants of different states; and between a state, or the citizens therof, and foreign states, citizens or subjects.

In all cases affecting ambassadors, other public ministers and consuls, and those in which a state shall be party, the supreme court shall have original jurisdiction. In all the other cases before mentioned, the supreme court shall have appellate jurisdiction, both as to law and fact, with such exceptions, and under such regulations, as the congress shall make.

The trial of all crimes, except in cases of impeachment, shall be by jury; and such trial shall be held in the state where the said crimes shall have been committed; but when not committed within any state, the trial shall be at such place or places as the congress may by law have directed.

Section 3. Treason against the United States, shall consist only in levying war against them, or in adhering to their enemies, giving them aid and comfort. No person shall be convicted of treason unless on the testimony of two witnesses to the same overt act, or on confession in open court.

The Congress shall have power to declare the punishment of treason, but no attainder of treason shall work corruption of blood, or forfeiture, except during the life of the person attainted.

Article IV

Section 1. Full faith and credit shall be given in each state to the public acts, records, and judicial proceedings of every other state. And the congress may by general laws prescribe the manner in which such acts, records, and proceedings shall be proved, and the effect thereof.

Section 2. The citizens of each state shall be entitled to all privileges and immunities of citizens in the several states.

A person charged in any state with treason, felony, or other crime, who shall flee from justice, and be found in another state, shall, on demand of the executive authority of the state from which he fled, be delivered up, to be removed to the state having jurisdiction of the crime.

No person held to service or labour in one state, under the laws thereof, escaping into another, shall, in consequence of any law or regulation therein, be discharged from such service or labour, but shall be delivered up on claim of the party to whom such service or labour may be due.

SECTION 3. New states may be admitted by the congress into this union; but no new state shall be formed or erected within the jurisdiction of any other state, nor any state be formed by the junction of two or more states, or parts of states, without the consent of the legislatures of the states concerned, as well as of the congress.

The congress shall have power to dispose of and make all needful rules and regulations respecting the territory or other property belonging to the United States; and nothing in this constitution shall be so construed as to prejudice any claims of the United States, or of any particular state.

SECTION 4. The United States shall guarantee to every state in this Union, a republican form of government, and shall protect each of them against invasion; and on application of the legislature, or of the executive (when the legislature cannot be convened) against domestic violence.

ARTICLE V

The congress, whenever two-thirds of both houses shall deem it necessary, shall propose amendments to this constitution, or, on the application of the legislatures of two-thirds of the several states, shall call a convention for proposing amendments, which, in either case, shall be valid to all intents and purposes, as part of this constitution, when ratified by the legislatures of three-fourths of the several states, or by conventions in three-fourths thereof, as the one or the other mode of ratification may be proposed by the congress: Provided, that no amendment which may be made prior to the year one thousand eight hundred and eight, shall in any manner affect the first and fourth clauses in the ninth section of the first article; and that no state, without its consent, shall be deprived of its equal suffrage in the senate.

ARTICLE VI

All debts contracted and engagements entered into, before the adoption of this constitution, shall be as ...d against the United States under this constitution, as under the confederation.

This constitution, and the laws of the United States which shall be made in pursuance thereof; and all treaties made, or which shall be made, under the authority of the United States, shall be the supreme law of the land; and the judges in every state shall be bound thereby, anything in the constitution or laws of any state to the contrary notwithstanding.

The senators and representatives before mentioned, and the members of the several states legislatures, and all executive and judicial officers, both of the United States and of the several states, shall be bound by oath or affirmation to support this constitution; but no religious test shall ever be required as a qualification to any office or public trust under the United States.

ARTICLE VII

The ratification of the convention of nine states shall be sufficient for the establishment of this constitution between the states so ratifying the same.

ARTICLES in addition to, and Amendment of the Constitution of the United States of America, proposed by Congress, and ratified by the Legislatures of the several States, pursuant to the fifth Article of the original Constitution.

AMENDMENT I [I-X adopted in 1791]

Congress shall make no law respecting an establishment of religion, or prohibiting the free exercise thereof; or abridg-

ing the freedom of speech, or of the press; or the right of the
people peaceably to assemble, and to petition the Government
for a redress of grievances.

AMENDMENT II

A well regulated Militia, being necessary to the security of
a free State, the right of the people to keep and bear Arms,
shall not be infringed.

AMENDMENT III

No Soldier shall, in time of peace be quartered in any
house, without the consent of the Owner, nor in time of war,
but in a manner to be prescribed by law.

AMENDMENT IV

The right of the people to be secure in their persons,
houses, papers, and effects, against unreasonable searches and
seizures, shall not be violated, and no Warrants shall issue, but
upon probable cause, supported by Oath or affirmation, and
particularly describing the place to be searched, and the persons or things to be seized.

AMENDMENT V

No person shall be held to answer for a capital, or otherwise infamous crime, unless on a presentment or indictment
of a Grand Jury, except in cases arising in the land or naval
forces, or in the Militia, when in actual service in time of War
or public danger; nor shall any person be subject for the
same offense to be twice put in jeopardy of life or limb; nor
shall be compelled in any criminal case to be a witness against
himself, nor be deprived of life, liberty, or property, without
due process of law; nor shall private property be taken for
public use, without just compensation.

AMENDMENT VI

In all criminal prosecutions, the accused shall enjoy the right to a speedy and public trial, by an impartial jury of the State and district wherein the crime shall have been committed, which district shall have been previously ascertained by law, and to be informed of the nature and cause of the accusation; to be confronted with the witnesses against him; to have compulsory process for obtaining witnesses in his favor, and to have the Assistance of Counsel for his defense.

AMENDMENT VII

In Suits at common law, where the value in controversy shall exceed twenty dollars, the right of trial by jury shall be preserved, and no fact tried by a jury, shall be otherwise re-examined in any Court of the United States, than according to the rules of the common law.

AMENDMENT VIII

Excessive bail shall not be required, nor excessive fines imposed, nor cruel and unusual punishments inflicted.

AMENDMENT IX

The enumeration in the Constitution, of certain rights, shall not be construed to deny or disparage others retained by the people.

AMENDMENT X

The powers not delegated to the United States by the Constitution, nor prohibited by it to the States, are reserved to the States respectively, or to the people.

AMENDMENT XI [adopted in 1798]

The Judicial power of the United States shall not be con-strued to extend to any suit in law or equity, commenced or prosecuted against one of the United States by Citizens of another State, or by Citizens or Subjects of any Foreign State.

AMENDMENT XII [adopted in 1804]

The Electors shall meet in their respective states, and vote by ballot for President and Vice-President, one of whom, at least, shall not be an inhabitant of the same state with them-selves; they shall name in their ballots the person voted for as President, and in distinct ballots the person voted for as Vice-President, and they shall make distinct lists of all persons voted for as President, and of all persons voted for as Vice-President, and of the number of votes for each, which lists they shall sign and certify, and transmit sealed to the seat of the government of the United States, directed to the President of the Senate;—The President of the Senate shall, in the presence of the Senate and House of Representatives, open all certificates and the votes shall then be counted;—The person having the greatest number of votes for President, shall be the President, if such number be a majority of the whole number of Electors appointed; and if no person have such majority, then from the persons having the highest numbers not exceeding three on the list of those voted for as President, the House of Representatives shall choose immediately, by ballot, the President. But in choosing the President, the votes shall be taken by states, the representation from each state having one vote; a quorum for this purpose shall consist of a member or members from two-thirds of the states, and a majority of all the states shall be necessary to a choice. And if the House of Representatives shall not choose a President whenever the right of choice shall devolve upon them, before the fourth day of March next following, then the Vice-Presi-